Dedication

··

This book is dedicated to all the martini drinkers and bartenders who stir, shake, and serve. To Jaclyn Marie and Ryan Foley and the rest of the tribe!

Acknowledgments

Allied Domecq Spirits USA –
    Robert Suffredini
Angostura International Ltd.
Anheuser-Busch, Inc. – Diane Burnell
Austin, Nichols & Co., Inc.
Bacardi USA, Inc.
Banta Book Group – Bob Christopher
Barton Incorporated
Branca Products Corporation
Brown-Forman Beverages Worldwide
Cairns & Associates, Inc.
Charles Jacquin et Cie., Inc. – Patricia
    Bornmann, John Cooper, Kevin O'Brien
Coco Lopez, Inc. – Jose Suarez, R. Jake
    Jacobsen
Crillon Importers – Michel Roux,
    Jerry Ciraulo
Dozortsev & Sons Enterprises, Ltd.
Dunwoodie Communications – Greg Cohen
Finlandia Vodka Americas, Inc. –
    Chester Brandes
Heaven Hill Distilleries, Inc.
Jim Beam Brands Worldwide, Inc.
Kobrand Corp.
Kratz & Jensen, Inc. – Christine Deussen,
    Alicia DiFolco
Major Peters Bloody Mary Mix
Manitowoc Ice, Inc. – Larry Hagman
Marie Brizard Wines and Spirits, USA
Miller Brewing Company – Joan Zitzke
Mott's USA – Jeff Polisoto
National Cherry Board – Cheryl Kroupa
Niche Marketing
Remy Amerique – Robert Rentsch,
    Oton Gomez

Schieffelin & Somerset – Jeff Pogash
Seagram North America – Robert Dubin,
    Arthur Shapiro
Skyy Spirits LLC
Steve Baron Communications
The Baddish Group – Laura Baddish
The Food Group – Mark Bloom
The Gang at Maker's Mark
Todhunter International, Inc.
Top Shelf Marketing – George and
    Kelly Borrello
UDV North America
Vita Mix
Waring Products – Joan Gioiella

Special thanks to Jimmy Zazzali, Matt Wojciak,
John Cowan, Michael Cammarano, Charles
Chop, Marvin Solomon, the Rinaldis (Millie
and Anthony), as well as Julie Christopher and
Loretta Natiello for putting this to paper.

In addition, to all those who submitted recipes
to www.bartender.com and the readers of
Bartender magazine.

A Short History of the Origins of the Martini

1. Made by bartender professor Jerry Thomas of San Francisco for a stranger on his way to Martinez. Made with gin, vermouth, bitters, dash of maraschino.

2. Made by a bartender in Martinez, California, for a gold miner who struck it rich. The miner ordered champagne for the house, but there was none. The bartender offered something better— "Martinez Special"—made with sauterne and gin. The rich miner spread the word, ordering throughout California a "Martinez Special."

3. Named after the British army rifle: The Martini and Henry. The rifle was known for its kick, like the first sip of gin and "it" ("it" being vermouth).

4. Named after Martini and Rossi vermouth, because it was first used in the drink, gin, and "it," with 1/2 gin and 1/2 Martini and Rossi vermouth.

5. At the Knickerbocker Hotel in the early 1900s, a bartender named Martini di Arma Tiggia mixed a martini using only a dry gin and only dry vermouth.

Instructions

All recipes have been alphabetized for your convenience.

1. Shake, stir, swirl, strain, or whatever. It's really up to you.

2. Some drinks (not many) have the same ingredients, but different brand names—pick your favorite.

3. If you have trouble finding an ingredient, omit it and go on with your life.

4. If the recipe does not have measurements, use your own taste.

5. We do not recommend flaming a drink.

6. Don't drink and drive.

7. Always use the "best" ingredients.

8. For more information: www.bartender.com

9. Vermouth: French = white/dry;
   Italian = red/sweet

10. Have a great life, enjoy your martini.

Publisher's Note: This book and the recipes contained herein are intended for those of a legal drinking age. Please drink responsibly and ensure you and your guests have a designated driver when consuming alcoholic beverages.

"007" Martini

1 oz. Gordon's vodka
1 oz. Gordon's gin
1/2 oz. Lillet Blanc

Rinse glass with extra dry vermouth. Garnish with lemon twist.

151 Martini Bacardi

Martini & Rossi Rosso
splash cranberry juice

Shaken and strained into a martini glass. Garnish with a twist.

1800 Carats Martini

Cuervo 1800
Grand Marnier
lime squeeze

Gatsby
Boca Raton, FL

1940s Classic Martini

Tangueray
Noilly Prat dry vermouth

Garnish with an olive.

Continental Café
Philadelphia, PA

1951 Martini

2 oz. Gordon's gin
splash Cointreau
anchovy stuffed olive

Rinse glass with Cointreau. Add the gin and olive.

24-Karrot Martini

Ketel One with a spicy baby carrot

Straight up or over ice.

A Bally Good Martini

2 oz. Bombay Sapphire
1/8 oz. dry vermouth
1/8 oz. Grand Marnier

Garnish with an orange twist.

Bally's
Las Vegas, NV

A Bentley Martini

1 oz. sweet vermouth
2 oz. Calvados

Place in shaker with good quantity of cube ice. Shake or stir to taste. Strain into "up" prechilled glass. Garnish with twist of lemon zest.

Tim Worstall
San Luis Obispo, CA

Peachini Martini

2 cups of fresh-skinned peaches
3 oz. vodka
small scoop of crushed ice

Blend till smooth.

Jill Stevens
Trabuco Canyon, CA

A.1 Martini

2 oz. dry gin
1 oz. Grand Marnier or Cointreau
tsp. lemon juice
1/2 tsp. grenadine

Shake and strain.

About That Time

2 1/2 oz. Alize
dash grenadine

Serve chilled in martini glass. Garnish with a
strawberry.

Iris Vourlatos
Email

Absolut Hurricane Warning

1 1/2 oz. Absolut vodka
2 oz. pineapple and cranberry juice

Garnish with maraschino cherry.

Hurricane Restaurant
Passagrille, FL

Absolut Legend Martini

Absolut vodka shaken with lime juice and
crème de mure.

Lot 61
New York, NY

Absolutly Fabulous Martini

1 1/4 oz. Absolut Citron vodka
1 1/4 oz. Absolut Kurant vodka
lemon twist for garnish

Stir with ice and strain into a chilled martini
glass. Garnish with lemon twist.

The Martini Club
Atlanta, GA

Acid Rain

1 part Rain vodka, chilled
1 part grapefruit juice, chilled

Strain into martini glass. Garnish with twist of
lime.

Acropolis Martini

1 3/4 oz. Smirnoff vodka
1/4 oz. Ouzo 12

Strain and garnish with a black olive.

Adam & Eve Martini

1 oz. dry gin
1 oz. Forbidden Fruit liqueur
1 oz. cognac
1 tsp. lemon juice

Shake and strain.

Addison Martini

1 oz. dry gin
1 1/2 oz. Martini & Rossi sweet vermouth

Shake and strain. Decorate with maraschino cherry.

Adios Amigos Martini

1 oz. dry gin
1/2 oz. brandy
1/2 oz. white rum
1/2 oz. Martini & Rossi sweet vermouth
1/2 oz. lemon juice

Shake and strain.

Admiral Martini

1 oz. bourbon
1 1/2 oz. dry vermouth
1/2 oz. fresh lemon juice
lemon twist

Shake liquid ingredients with ice. Strain into chilled cocktail glass. Drop in lemon twist.

Adonis Cocktail

1 oz. fino sherry (Tio Pepe or La Ina)
1 oz. Martini & Rossi sweet vermouth
1 oz. fresh squeezed orange juice
dash Angostura bitters

Shake all ingredients with ice. Strain into chilled cocktail glass. Garnish with orange peel.

Dale DeGroff
Email, www.kingcocktail.com

Affinity Martini

1 oz. scotch
1 oz. dry vermouth
1 oz. sweet vermouth
2 dashes Angostura bitters

Stir liquid ingredients with ice. Strain into chilled glass. Garnish with maraschino cherry.

Affinity #2 Martini

1 oz. scotch
1 oz. dry sherry
1 oz. ruby port
2 dashes Angostura or orange bitters
maraschino cherry

After the Frost Martini

Mission Hill Grand Reserve Ice wine
Bombay gin or Finlandia vodka

Garnish with frozen Riesling grapes. Serve in
an ice martini glass set over dry ice.

*900 West in the Canadian Pacific Hotel
Vancouver, BC*

After-Dinner Martini

2 oz. Stolichnaya Kafya
1/4 oz. Stolichnaya Vanil or Stoli Zinamon

Garnish with several coffee beans.

Afterglow Martini

1 part melon liqueur
2 parts vodka
1 part orange juice

Serve very cold with a dash of lemon.

Agatini

2 shots Absolut Citron
splash Chambord

Strain into sugar-rimmed martini glass.
Garnish with a twist.

Patty Nolletti Restaurant
Rochester, NY

Agnese's Goldenrod Martini

Tanqueray gin
Martini & Rossi extra dry vermouth
drop of Grand Marnier

Add a rod of lemon and orange.

Orso's
Chicago, IL

Air Traffic Control

1 part Courvoisier VSOP
1 part crème de menthe
lemon twist

The Windsock Bar & Grill
San Diego, CA

Alaska Martini

2 oz. dry gin
1 1/2 oz. lemon juice
1 tsp. caster sugar

Shake and strain into tall glass. Float on top 1
tsp. raspberry syrup or 1 tsp. crème de cassis.

Alaska Martini II

1 1/2 dry gin
1/2 Yellow Chartreuse

Shake and strain.

Algonquin Martini

2 oz. blended whiskey
1 oz. dry vermouth
1 oz. unsweetened pineapple juice

Shake ingredients with ice. Strain into chilled
cocktail glass or serve over ice cubes in an
old-fashioned glass.

Algonquin Hotel
New York, NY

Alize Caribbean Martini

2 oz. Alize
1/2 oz. Bacardi Limon

Fill shaker with ice, add above ingredients, cover, and shake. Strain ice-cold into martini glass. Garnish with lemon slice.

Alize Martini

1 1/2 oz. Alize
1/2 oz. Absolut

Fill shaker with ice, add above ingredients, cover martini shaker, and shake. Strain ice-cold into martini glass. Garnish with thin slice of lemon.

Alize Nectar

1 1/2 oz. Alize
1/2 oz. amaretto
1/2 oz. rum
1/2 oz. vodka
1 oz. grenadine

Mix ingredients in shaker. Shake and strain into tall glass.

Andrew Thompson
Rock & Kath's Sawmill

Alize Passionate Martini

2 oz. Alize
1/2 oz. Absolut
1/2 oz. cranberry juice

Alize Red Passion Martini

2 1/2 oz. Alize Red Passion
1 oz. super premium vodka

Fill martini shaker 3/4 with ice. Add above ingredients. Strain ice-cold into martini glass. Garnish with relatively thin slice of lime.

Alize de France

Alize Tropical Martini

2 oz. Alize
1/2 oz. Malibu

Fill shaker with ice, add above ingredients, cover, and shake. Garnish with maraschino cherry.

All Too Important Martini

touch of dry vermouth (1 part to 8 parts
    Tangueray gin)
2 1/2 oz. Tangueray gin
2 olives for garnish

Pour vermouth into a chilled glass and swirl it
around. Dump the vermouth into the sink.
Chill the Tangueray gin until cold and strain
into the glass. Garnish with the two olives
skewered on a pick.

Johnny Love's
San Francisco, CA

Allies Martini

1 oz. gin
1 oz. dry vermouth
2 dashes Kummel

Stir or shake with ice. Strain into chilled glass.

Aloha Martini

2 oz. Smirnoff vodka
1/4 oz. pineapple juice
1/4 oz. apricot brandy

Chill, strain, and garnish with a pineapple wedge.

Alternative Martini

2 oz. Absolut Citron
1/2 oz. Grand Marnier

Chill and strain into martini glass. Garnish with lemon twist.

James Allison, Jr.
Boise, ID

Alternatini Martini

3 oz. Tangueray Sterling vodka
splash Martini & Rossi extra dry vermouth
splash Martini & Rossi Rosso vermouth
1/2 oz. white crème de cacao

Rim martini glass in chocolate fudge
Garnish with Reese's Peanut Butter Cup.

Jilly's Bistro
Chicago, IL

Ambassador Martini

2 oz. Smirnoff vodka
dash melon liqueur
dash orange juice

Chill, strain, and garnish with an orange wheel.

Amber Dream Martini

2 parts dry gin
1 part Italian vermouth
dash orange bitters
3 dashes Yellow Chartreuse

Shake.

Amber Martini

1 oz. vodka
1/2 oz. amaretto
1/2 oz. hazelnut liqueur

Chill, strain, and serve in a chilled martini glass.

American Pie Martini

2 oz. Skyy vodka
1/4 oz. Stoli Zinamon
1/4 oz. Calvados

Garnish with a small wedge of apple. Dip side of the apple slice in cinnamon. Cut a small slice into the apple so that it fits onto the rim of the glass.

Americano

2 parts Martini & Rossi sweet vermouth
1 part Campari

Pour over ice and stir. Serve in tall glass
topped with club soda.

Amethyst Martini

2 oz. Ketel One vodka
1/2 oz. Campari
1/2 oz. Chambord
splash lime juice

Amides Martini

2 oz. Stolichnaya vodka
1/2 oz. Godiva liqueur
splash Frangelico

Garnish with an almond or hazelnut.

Angel Martini

1 1/2 oz. Ketel One vodka
1/2 oz. Frangelico

Shake ingredients with ice. Strain into a
chilled martini glass.

Angelina Classy Lady

2 oz. Bacardi Limon
1/8 oz. Rose's lime juice
1/2 oz. 7-Up or Sprite
1/8 oz. Martini & Rossi extra dry vermouth

An Irish Mexican in Russian Vanilla Fields

1 oz. Stoli Vanil
1/2 oz. Baileys Irish Cream
1/2 oz. Kahlúa
half and half
scoop vanilla ice cream
dash cinnamon

Mix all ingredients except cinnamon in blender.

Stephanie Meagher-Garcia
Chilli's Bar & Grill, Miami, FL

Annawanna/Tropical Martini

1 oz. Malibu coconut rum
1/2 oz. pineapple juice
splash Rose's lime juice
dash salt

Shake, add ice, shake again, and strain into chilled martini glasses. Garnish with fruit.

Antini Martini

2 oz. Stolichnaya Cristall vodka
1/2 oz. Lillet Rouge
burnt orange twist for garnish

Shake with ice and strain into a chilled martini
glass. Garnish with ice burnt orange twist.

Harry Denton's Starlight Room
San Francisco, CA

Apple Jack Martini

Muddled apple and cinnamon shaken with
Ketel One vodka.

Served with a sugared cinnamon rim.

Lot 61
New York, NY

Apple Kiss Martini

3/4 oz. vodka
3/4 oz. sour apple pucker
1/2 scoop ice
splash sour mix

Blend and serve frozen in chilled martini
glass. Rim with lime green sugar. Garnish
with wedge of apple.

Pamela Conaway
Hurricane Restaurant, Passagrille, FL

Apple Martini

1 1/2 oz. Glacier vodka
1/2 part Schoenauer Apfel schnapps
dash cinnamon

Garnish with a slice of apple.

Apple of My Eye

1 oz. Rain vodka
3/4 oz. apple brandy
1/4 oz. lime juice
1/4 oz. grenadine

Chill and serve straight up in martini glass.

Appletini

1 1/2 oz. Ketel One vodka
2 oz. DeKuyper Sour Apple Pucker

Served in chilled martini glass. Garnish with
a round slice of apple.

Bobby McGee's
San Bernardino, CA

Appletini II

3 parts Bombay gin
1 part Midori
splash pineapple
splash sweet and sour

Shake hard with cut up apple chunks. Garnish
with apple slice.

Mike Simpson
Il Fornaio, San Diego, CA

Apres-Skitini

2 oz. Stoli Zinamon
splash mulled cider

Serve in a warm martini glass with a cinnamon
stick.

Apricot Martini

1 part Godiva liqueur
1 part Absolut vodka
1 part apricot brandy

Combine with ice, shake well. Serve chilled
with a maraschino cherry.

April Rain Martini

1 1/2 oz. Rain vodka
3 dashes triple sec and sour mix
splash cranberry juice

Shake with ice. Strain into martini glass.
Garnish with lemon slice.

Aquaman Martini

1 oz. aquavit
1 oz. gin
dash dry vermouth

Stir with ice, garnish with olive.

Aquarelle Martini

2 oz. Bacardi Limon
1 oz. Ketel One vodka
1/2 oz. Prunella Sauvage (local product)
2 drops blue curacao
lemon twist

John Hyde, Bartender
The Watergate Hotel, Washington, DC

Aquavit Martini

3 oz. O.P. Anderson aquavit
few drops of dry vermouth

Arcadiana Bartender's Favorite Martini

2 oz. Absolut Citron
sweet vermouth
lime wedge

Shake vermouth and lime wedge, add vodka.
Shake and strain.

Stephanie Guidry
Acadiana's Catfish Shark, Lafayette, LA

Aristicratico

Cuervo 1800 tequila
hint of Grand Marnier
jalapeno

No. 18
New York, NY

Arlenie Martini

1 oz. gin
2 oz. Limoncello
1 oz. Frangelico
dash rum

Shake with ice and strain into 4 oz. martini glass.

Steve Visakay
Vintage Cocktail Shakers

Army Cocktail Martini

2 oz. dry gin
1/2 oz. sweet vermouth
orange peel

Artillery Martini

2 oz. gin
1 oz. sweet vermouth

Shake ingredients with ice. Strain into chilled glass.

Astoria Martini

1 1/2 oz. dry gin
3/4 oz. dry vermouth
dash orange bitters
green olive

Atta Boy Martini

2 oz. dry gin
1/2 oz. dry vermouth
2 dashes grenadine

Attitude-Tini

Absolut Citron vodka
Cointreau
fresh lemon juice in sugar rimmed glass

The Diner on Sycamore
Cincinnati, OH

Atty Martini

2 oz. dry gin
1/2 oz. dry vermouth
2 dashes crème de violette
twist of lemon peel

Autumn Martini

Stoli Zinamon
flavor with amaretto liqueur
orange slice

Renaissance Atlanta Hotel
Atlanta, GA

Aviator Martini

Tangueray citrus vodka
splash cranberry juice
lemon mix
lemon wedge

The Windsock Bar & Grill
San Diego, CA

B.R. Martini

1 1/2 oz. Stoli Vanil
1/2 oz. Kahlúa
splash cream

Garnish with chocolate mint stir.

John Del Giorno
Mirage, Las Vegas, NV

B.V.D. Martini

3/4 oz. Bacardi light rum
3/4 oz. dry vermouth
3/4 oz. Dubonnet

Stir ingredients with ice. Strain into chilled glass.

Babe Ruth Martini

1/2 oz. Absolut
3/4 oz. dark crème de cacao
3/4 oz. butterscotch schnapps

Fill mixing glass with ice. Stir and strain into chilled glass. Garnish with miniature Baby Ruth.

Chris "Barman" Davis
Lodge at Lakeview, Austin, TX

Bacardi Dry Martini

2 oz. Bacardi light rum
1/2 oz. Martini & Rossi dry vermouth

Shake with ice and strain.

Bacardi Limon Martini

2 oz. Bacardi Limon
3/4 oz. Martini & Rossi extra dry vermouth
splash cranberry juice

Shake with ice and strain into chilled martini
glasses. Garnish with lemon twist.

Bacardi Spice Caribbean Martini

2 1/2 oz. Bacardi spice rum
1/2 oz. crème de banana

Shake and strain over ice. Serve straight up.
Garnish with pineapple wedge or cube.

Bacardi Sweet Martini

2 oz. Bacardi light rum
Martini & Rossi sweet vermouth

Bad Apple Martini

1 1/2 oz. Absolut Citron
1/2 oz. Berentzen Apfel liqueur
2 drops Tabasco sauce

Chill, shake, and strain Absolut into chilled martini glass. Pour Berentzen down side of glass. Pour two drops of Tabasco in center. Garnish with apple slice.

The Country Barrel Inn
Crosswicks, NJ

Bailey's Chocolate Martini

1 1/2 part Baileys
1 part Stolichnaya vodka
1/2 part crème de cacao

Garnish with a maraschino cherry.

Ballantine's Cocktail

1 1/2 oz. dry gin
3/4 oz. French vermouth
dash orange bitters
dash Pernod

Ballet Russe

2 oz. Stolichnaya vodka
1/4 oz. Chambord
1/4 oz. sour mix

The Diner on Sycamore
Cincinnati, OH

Bambou's Limon Martini

1/2 oz. Martini & Rossi extra dry vermouth
2 oz. Bacardi Limon
1 oz. Midori
lemon twist

Reebok Sports Club

Banana Martini

2 1/2 oz. Gordon's vodka
1/4 oz. crème de banana
splash extra dry vermouth

Garnish with caramelized banana.

Banana Split Martini

Finlandia Arctic Cranberry, chilled
1/4 oz. banana liqueur
1/4 oz. Chambord

Finlandia Vodka Americas, Inc.
New York, NY

Banzai Martini

2 3/4 oz. Skyy vodka
1/4 oz. sake

Rinse glass with Martini & Rossi extra dry vermouth. Garnish with Japanese pickled plum and shiso.

Betelnut
San Francisco, CA

Barbarella

2 oz. vodka
splash vermouth
Gorgonzola stuffed olives

Wolfgang Puck Express
Walt Disney World Resort, FL

Barbed Wire

2 1/2 oz. vodka
1/4 oz. Martini & Rossi Rosso vermouth
splash Pernod
splash Chambord

Garnish with a maraschino cherry.

Harris'
San Francisco, CA

Barnum Martini

1 1/2 oz. gin
1/2 oz. apricot brandy
4 dashes Angostura bitters
1/4 tsp. fresh lemon juice

Shake ingredients with ice. Strain into chilled glass.

Baron Martini

1 1/2 oz. dry gin
1/2 oz. French vermouth
1/4 oz. orange curacao
1/4 oz. sweet vermouth
twist of lemon peel

Barry Martini

1 1/2 oz. dry gin
3/4 oz. sweet vermouth
dash Angostura bitters
white crème de menthe

Stir into glass. Float crème de menthe on top. Garnish with twist of lemon peel.

Bean Machine

Finlandia vodka, chilled
1/2 oz. Kahlúa

Finlandia Vodka Americas, Inc.
New York, NY

Beauty Spot Martini

1 oz. gin
1/2 oz. dry vermouth
1/2 oz. sweet vermouth
1 tsp. fresh orange juice
dash grenadine

Put grenadine in bottom of chilled glass.
Shake remaining ingredients with ice. Strain
into glass—don't stir.

Becco's Martini

1 1/2 oz. Stoli Ohranj vodka
1 1/2 oz. Campari
1/2 oz. Martini & Rossi sweet vermouth
orange peel

Reebok Sports Club

Bee's Knees Martini

2 oz. dry gin
1 oz. lemon juice
1 oz. clear honey

Shake and strain.

Bel-Air Martini

1/2 oz. sherry
2 oz. vodka

Garnish with lemon twist.

Bellini Martini

Stolichnaya vodka
fresh white peach puree
zest of lemon

Martini's
New York, NY

Bennett Cocktail Martini

1 1/2 oz. gin
2 tsp. fresh lime juice
1 tsp. powered sugar
2 dashes Angostura or orange bitters

Shake ingredients with ice. Strain into chilled glass.

Beri-Beri Nice

1 part Stoli Strasberi vodka
1 part Stoli Razberi vodka
splash Chambord

Garnish with fresh raspberry.

Peggy Howell
Cotati Yacht Club & Saloon, Cotati, CA

Bermuda Highball Martini

1 oz. gin
1 oz. dry vermouth
1 oz. brandy
cold club soda or ginger ale
lemon twist

Put 2 to 3 ice cubes in chilled glass. Add gin, vermouth, and brandy. Top with club soda or ginger ale, stirring gently. Drop in lemon.

Bermudiana Rose

2 oz. Cork dry gin
1/4 oz. apricot brandy
1/4 oz. grenadine
1/4 oz. lemon juice

Shake.

Berry Berry Martini

2 oz. Beefeater gin
1/2 oz. cranberry cocktail

Shake and strain into chilled martini glass. Garnish with a fresh berry.

Berry Mocha Martini

1 1/2 oz. Stoli Razberi
1/4 oz. Godiva chocolate liqueur
1/4 oz. Kahlúa

Garnish with raspberries or chocolate.

Keely Kurtas
Allentown Bartender School, Whitehall, PA

Big Apple Martini

3 oz. Finlandia vodka
1/2 oz. green apple schnapps
1 1/2 oz. sweet and sour mix

Garnish with paper-thin wafer of green apple.

Bubble Lounge
San Francisco, CA

Bijou Cocktail Martini

1 oz. gin
1 oz. sweet vermouth
1 oz. Green Chartreuse
dash orange bitters

Stir liquid ingredients with ice. Strain into
chilled glass. Garnish with maraschino cherry.

Bikini Martini

1/3 Absolut Citron
1/3 Malibu rum
1/3 pineapple juice

Garnish with pineapple flag.

Key Club Hollywood
Hollywood, CA

Bitch on Wheels

Bombay gin
Martini & Rossi extra dry vermouth
Pernod
white crème de menthe

Shake with ice and strain into chilled martini glass.

Stars
San Francisco, CA

Bitchin' Martini

1 1/2 oz. gin
1/2 oz. dry vermouth
1-2 dashes crème de menthe
1-2 dashes Pernod
twist of lemon

Stir and serve.

Bittersweet Martini

1 1/2 oz. dry vermouth
1 1/2 oz. sweet vermouth
dash Angostura bitters
dash orange bitters
orange twist

Shake liquid ingredients with ice. Strain into chilled glass. Drop in orange twist.

Black Currant Martini

1 oz. Godiva liqueur
1 oz. Seagram's gin
1/4 oz. crème de cassis
1/4 oz. lemon juice
1/4 oz. lime juice

Combine ingredients with ice. Shake well, and strain into cocktail glass. Garnish with maraschino cherry.

Black Eyed "P"

Absolut Peppar vodka

Garnish with black olives.

Cecilia's
Breckenridge, CO

Black Magic

Jägermeister
vodka

Chill and serve straight up.

Black Martini

1 1/2 oz. Absolut Kurant
splash Chambord

Stir ingredients and serve straight up or over ice.

Continental Café
Philadelphia, PA

Black Martini II

Absolut vodka
Kahlúa
shot of chilled espresso
whisk of cream

Serve in oversized, chilled stem.

The Bitter End

Black Stallion Martini

2 oz. Smirnoff vodka
dash Romana Black sambuca

Chill, strain, and sprinkle with 3 espresso beans.

Black Tie Martini

1 1/2 oz. Skyy vodka
spritz Campari
spritz Chivas
2 cocktail onions
1 black olive

Blackberry Martini

Stoli Vanil
Chambord

Tunnel Bar Raphael
Providence, RI

Blackthorn Martini

1 1/2 oz. sloe gin
1 oz. sweet vermouth
2 dashes bitters

Stir and strain into chilled glass. Garnish with
lemon twist.

Blazing Iris

2 oz. Vincent vodka
1/2 oz. Chambord

Combine ingredients, shake, and strain into a
martini glass. Garnish with caramelized lime
pinwheels.

Andy Porter
Van Gogh's Restaurant & Bar, Atlanta, GA

Bleu Martini

Fris vodka
dry vermouth

Garnish with olives stuffed with bleu cheese.

Bleeding Heart Martini

Chill bottle of Campari in freezer until it gets
syrupy. Wet and chill cocktail glass in freezer
as well. Pour 6 oz. Ketel One vodka into mixing glass with ice. Swirl and strain into chilled
cocktail glass. Slowly pour Campari around
rim of glass. Garnish with a black olive.

Thomas Rozycki
Bloomsburg, PA

Blenton Martini

1 1/2 oz. dry gin
3/4 oz. dry vermouth
dash Angostura bitters
twist of lemon peel

Blimlet Martini

2 oz. dry gin
2 oz. Rose's lime juice
1 oz. lemon juice
1/2 oz. crème de cassis

Blonde Martini

Bombay Sapphire
enlivened with Lillet Blonde

*Brasserie Jo Martini's
Chicago, IL*

Blood and Sand Martini

3/4 oz. scotch
3/4 oz. cherry brandy
3/4 oz. sweet vermouth
3/4 oz. fresh orange juice

Shake ingredients with ice. Strain into chilled glass.

Blood Ohranj Martini

3 parts Stoli Ohranj vodka
1 part Campari
splash club soda

Stir ingredients with ice.

Bloodhound Martini

1 oz. gin
1/2 oz. dry vermouth
1/2 oz. sweet vermouth
1/2 oz. strawberry liqueur

Shake liquid ingredients with ice. Strain into chilled glass. Garnish with a strawberry.

Bloody Martini

2 oz. Smirnoff vodka
dash tomato juice
generous shake of Worcestershire sauce and
    Tabasco

Chill and strain into a martini glass. Top with freshly grated horseradish and garnish with a lime.

Blue Dolphin Martini

2 oz. Finlandia vodka, chilled
1/4 oz. blue curacao
1/4 oz. Grand Marnier
1 oz. grapefruit juice
2 drops Rose's lime juice

Blue Eyed Tomcat

Bombay Sapphire gin martini dressed with
Tomolives.

Cecilia's
Breckenridge, CO

Blue Gordon's Martini

Gordon's vodka
blue curacao
twist of lemon

Blue Water

2 oz. Skyy vodka
1/4 oz. blue curacao

Shake. Serve up or on the rocks.

Saba Blue Water Café
Austin, TX

Blue Lagoon Martini

1 1/4 oz. Bacardi Limon
1/2 oz. blue curacao
1/4 oz. dry vermouth

Garnish with strawberry or olives.

Alex Refojo
Club Mystique, Miami, FL

Blue Martini

1 oz. Stoli Limonnaya
1 oz. Stoli Razberi
splash sour mix
dash curacao

Garnish with lemon twist.

Blue Monday Martini

1 1/2 oz. Smirnoff vodka
3/4 oz. triple sec
dash blue curacao

Chill, strain, and garnish with an orange slice.

Blue Period Martini

Absolut vodka
Leyden gin
blue curacao
pineapple juice
splash Sprite

Martini Club
Atlanta, GA

Blue Room Martini

4 oz. Stoli Persik
splash sour mix
splash blue curacao

Shake and add twist.

Blue Sapphire Martini

splash dry vermouth
3 oz. Bombay Sapphire gin
1 oz. blue curacao

Stir with ice and strain into a chilled martini glass. Garnish with a maraschino cherry.

The Mandarin
San Francisco, CA

Blue Shark Martini

1 1/2 oz. vodka
1 1/2 oz. tequila
1/2 oz. blue curacao

Shake ingredients with ice. Strain into chilled martini glass or over ice.

Blue Skyy Martini

2 1/2 oz. Skyy vodka
splash blue curacao

Stir with ice and strain into chilled martini glass.

Compass Rose
San Francisco, CA

Blues Martini

1/2 oz. Ketel One vodka
1/2 oz. Bombay Sapphire gin
few drops blue curacao

Stir gently with ice. Serve straight up or over ice.

Bobby Burns Martini

1 1/2 oz. scotch
1 1/2 oz. sweet vermouth
1 1/2 tsp. Benedictine

Stir and strain into chilled glass. Garnish with lemon twist.

Bombay Martini

3 oz. Bombay gin
splash of Martini & Rossi dry vermouth

Garnish with bleu cheese olive.

Gibson's
Chicago, IL

Bonnie Prince Martini

1 1/2 oz. dry gin
1/2 oz. Lillet
1/4 oz. Drambuie

Bookmark

Ketel One vodka
dash of Chambord

Garnish with a Tomolive.

Boomerang Martini

4 parts dry gin
1 part French vermouth
1 part Italian vermouth
2 dashes maraschino cherry juice
twist of lemon peel

Boru Martini

Boru Original vodka
splash Boru orange or citrus vodka

Fill shaker with ice. Shake gently and strain
into chilled martini glass. Garnish with
orange or lemon peel.

Boston Bullet Martini

2 oz. dry gin
1/2 oz. dry vermouth
almond-stuffed green olive

Boticelli Martini

1 1/4 oz. Bombay Sapphire gin
1 1/4 oz. Ketel One vodka

Garnish with goat cheese stuffed olive.

Kevin Jason
Restorante Primavera, Millis, MA

Bottlegger Martini

Bombay gin
Southern Comfort
lemon twist

Chianti
Houston, TX

Bowery

Equal parts:
    Godiva liqueur
    Campari
    Ketel One vodka

Stir and serve.

Boxer Martini

2 oz. Absolut vodka
1 oz. Absolut Peppar
1/2 oz. Dubonnet Blanc (or vermouth)

Brandied Madeira Martini

1 oz. brandy
1 oz. Madeira
1/2 oz. dry vermouth

Stir with ice. Strain into chilled glass over ice
cubes. Garnish with lemon twist.

Brave Cow Martini

1 1/2 oz. gin
1/2 oz. coffee liqueur

Chill and strain into a chilled martini glass.

Brazil Cocktail Martini

1 1/2 oz. dry vermouth
1 1/2 oz. dry sherry
dash Angostura bitters
dash Pernod or other anise-flavored liqueur

Stir and strain into chilled glass. Garnish with lemon twist.

Breakfast Martini

Orange marmalade shaken with Stoli Ohranj and zest.

Lot 61
New York, NY

Brit Martini

Beefeater gin
blended with Pimm's #1
cucumber slice

Polo Lounge
Windsor Court Hotel, New Orleans, LA

Bronx Golden

Beefeater gin
dry vermouth
sweet vermouth
orange juice
egg yolk

Bronx Martini

Beefeater gin
Martini & Rossi extra dry vermouth
Martini & Rossi Rosso vermouth
orange juice
twist of lemon

Mr. Babbington's
New York, NY

Bronx Terrace Cocktail

1 1/2 oz. gin
3/4 oz. fresh lime juice
1/2 oz. dry vermouth
maraschino cherry

Shake with ice. Strain into chilled glass.
Garnish with maraschino cherry.

Brown Cocktail Martini

1 oz. light rum
1 oz. gin
3/4 oz. dry vermouth

Stir ingredients with ice. Strain into chilled glass.

Buckeye Martini

2 oz. Smirnoff vodka
1/2 oz. dry vermouth

Strain into glass. Garnish with black olive.

Buff Martini

5 parts Finlandia vodka
1 part Baileys Irish Cream
1 part Kahlúa

Stir gently with ice and strain. Add a sprinkle of freshly ground coffee or cinnamon.

Bulldog

1 1/2 oz. Beefeater gin
1 1/2 oz. orange juice

Stir juice and gin over ice in collins glass. Fill with ginger ale. Garnish with maraschino cherry or orange.

Bunny Hug Martini

1 oz. dry gin
1 oz. Pernod
1 oz. whiskey

Shake and strain.

Burnt Martini

1 1/2 oz. Beefeater gin
splash scotch

Shake with ice, strain, and serve with lemon twist.

Anita Sholdice
Qualicum Beach, BC

Cabaret Cocktail

2 oz. dry gin
1/4 oz. dry vermouth
1/4 oz. Benedictine
2 dashes Angostura bitters

Garnish with maraschino cherry.

Cabinieri

1 oz. Galliano
1 oz. Cointreau (or triple sec)
1 egg yolk

Pour liqueurs first into mixing glass. Crack egg and separate yolk from egg white. Add yolk to mixing glass. Add orange juice. Fill with ice and shake vigorously until all ingredients are fully integrated and mixture is well chilled. Strain into cocktail glass. Garnish with orange wheel.

Frederick C. Thomas
Long Island City, NY

Cajun King

1 1/2 oz. Absolut Peppar
3 drops cinnamon schnapps
splash Rose's lime juice

Garnish with jalapeno.

Cajun King Martini

1-2 dashes dry vermouth
1/2 oz. Absolut Citron
1 1/2 oz. Absolut Peppar

Small jalapeno peppers for garnish.

Cajun Martini

2 oz. Stoli Pertsovka
1/2 oz. dry vermouth

Garnish with a jalapeno pepper.

Cajun Martini II

Absolut Peppar vodka
dry vermouth

Garnish with Tomolives.

Cajun Martini III

1 seedless hot chili pepper in a bottle of
    vodka. Let sit for 24 hours. Soak olives in
    Tabasco for 10 minutes.
1 1/2 oz. hot chili pepper vodka

Dust rim with salt and pepper. Garnish with
hot olives.

Martini Message Board
Ft. Wayne, IN

Calisay Cocktail Martini

1 1/2 oz. Calisay
1 1/2 oz. sweet vermouth
1/4 tsp. fresh lime juice
1/2 tsp. powdered sugar

Shake ingredients with ice. Strain into chilled glass.

Calypso Splash

Leyden dry gin
blue curacao
splash of pineapple

Red Lobster
Memphis, TN

Campari Viceroy

2 oz. Campari
1/2 oz. Disaronno amaretto
1/2 oz. Southern Comfort
pineapple juice
orange juice

Shake well and serve over ice in a highball glass.

Campari Margie

3 parts Campari
1 part triple sec
1 part sour mix
dash Rose's lime juice

Shake and serve straight up in a chilled martini glass.

Campartini

2 oz. Campari
2 oz. Stoli Ohranj
dash Rose's lime juice
splash orange juice

Shaken, not stirred. Serve in a chilled martini glass with an orange slice.

Campton Cosmo Martini

1 1/2 oz. Absolut Citron vodka
1/4 oz. Tuaca
splash cranberry juice
1/2 oz. lemon juice
1 kumquat for garnish

Stir with ice and strain into a chilled martini glass. Garnish with the kumquat.

Campton Cure Martini

1 oz. Absolut Citron vodka
1/2 oz. Cointreau
3 squeezes lime juice
splash cranberry juice

Stir with ice and strain into a chilled martini glass.

Campton Place Hotel
San Francisco, CA

Candy-Cane Martini

vodka
green crème de menthe

Serve in a sugar-rimmed glass.

Cantini

Skyy vodka
Canton ginger liqueur

Garnish with candied ginger. Serve straight up in an oversized chilled stem. Shaken, not stirred.

Canton Martini

2 oz. Grey Goose vodka
1/2 oz. Grand Marnier
1/2 oz. Canton ginger liqueur

Shake vigorously. Garnish with a candied ginger slice.

Brad Nelson
56 West, Chicago, IL

Capital "G" Martini

Gordon's vodka
vermouth with Tomolive

Capoutini

2 oz. Leyden dry gin
splash raspberry puree

Garnish with 3 or 4 raspberries.

Jacques Capsouto
Capsouto Restaurant, New York, NY

Caprice Martini

1 1/2 oz. dry gin
1/2 oz. dry vermouth
1/2 oz. Benedictine
dash orange bitters

Cardamom Martini

Muddle 8/9 cardamom seeds with a large dash of sugar syrup and a large pour of Belvedere vodka.

Shake well. Strain through a sieve into a martini glass. Garnish with 3 cardamom seeds, if you can find them.

Ben Pundole, General Manager
Lot 61, New York, NY

Caribe Martini

1 oz. Mount Gay rum
1 oz. Bacardi
touch of pineapple

No. 18
New York, NY

Carnival Martini

vodka
fresh lime
orange juice

Coconut Grove
San Francisco, CA

Carroll Cocktail Martini

1 1/2 oz. brandy
3/4 oz. sweet vermouth

Stir liquid ingredients with ice. Strain into chilled glass. Garnish with maraschino cherry.

Cary Grant

2 1/2 oz. Luksusowa potato vodka
   (Polish vodka)
splash Tio Pepe (dry sherry)
1/2 oz. fresh lime juice

Rinse glass with Martini & Rossi extra dry vermouth.

Balboa
San Francisco, CA

Casino Cocktail

2 oz. gin
2 dashes Angostura bitters
1/4 oz. maraschino cherry juice
1/4 oz. lemon juice

Catalina Martini

2 1/2 oz. Gordon's vodka
1/2 oz. peach schnapps
1/2 oz. extra dry vermouth

Garnish with lemon twist soaked in Grand Marnier.

Catherine the Great Martini

Mixture of Absolut, Cointreau, and a dash of Framboise well shaken and topped with champagne.

Cecilia's Bold

Absolut Peppar
Beefeater gin
Italian dry vermouth
Chicago-style pepper

Cecilia's
Breckenridge, CO

Celebrity Martini

2 1/2 oz. gin
1 oz. Alize
1/2 oz. Grand Marnier

Rinse martini glass with Rose's lime cordial.
Shake remaining ingredients and strain into
glass. Garnish with lemon and lime twist.

Chris Golz
Forbidden Fruit, Long Beach, CA

Celtic Martini

Equal parts:
    Celtic Crossing
    lemon vodka

Garnish with a lemon twist.

Celtic Continental

Celtic Crossing
dash of Chambord
splash of peach schnapps

Shake and serve chilled in a martini glass.

Center of the Universe Martini

vodka
Coke
splash coffee
splash kiwi-strawberry
splash tonic
splash chocolate milk

Sasha Nicholas
Princeton, NJ

Champagne Martini

1 oz. Finlandia vodka
1/4 oz. Chambord
DeKuyper Peachtree schnapps
Korbel Brut champagne

Chill a martini glass. Fill a spray bottle with Peachtree schnapps. In martini shaker add ice, Finlandia, and Chambord. Liberally fill inner surface of martini glass with schnapps. Add contents of cocktail shaker and fill remainder of glass with cold champagne. Float one petal from a red rose on the surface and serve.

Craig Gilbert, F&B VP; Barrie Levin, Sommelier;
Dan Collins, Beverage Manager
Rio Suite Hotel and Casino, Las Vegas, NV

Champagne Royale de Martini

1 1/2 oz. premium vodka
1 oz. Veuve Clicquot Yellow Label champagne
1/2 oz. Chambord raspberry liqueur

Stir with ice and strain into a chilled martini glass. Garnish with lemon twist.

Tongue & Groove
Atlanta, GA

Chartrini Martini

vodka
dash Chartreuse

Chatterly Martini

2 oz. dry gin
1/2 oz. dry vermouth
1/4 oz. orange curacao

Cheap Thrill

DeKuyper Thrilla Vanilla liqueur
splash vodka

Serve very cold with the glass lightly drizzled with chocolate syrup. Top drink with a touch of whipped cream and cinnamon.

Chekhov Coffee Martini

Stoli Kafya with Romana Black served straight up.

Chelsea Sidecar

1 oz. Beefeater gin
1/8 oz. triple sec
1/8 oz. lime juice

Cheri Lace Martini

Equal parts:
    Cheri-Beri Pucker schnapps
    DeKuyper Thrilla Vanilla liqueur
splash vodka

Drop of chocolate syrup in the bottom. Rim glass with powered sugar.

Mindy Moller
Shake-Up Your Martini

Cherry Kiss

1 oz. Vincent vodka
1/2 oz. maraschino cherry juice
2 oz. pineapple juice
2 dashes grenadine

Combine ingredients, shake, and strain into a martini glass. Top with a bit of grated nutmeg.

Dale DeGroff
New York, NY

Cherry Ripe Martini

Combine:
1 1/2 oz. Smirnoff vodka
1/2 oz. cherry brandy
1/2 oz. brandy

Strain and garnish with a maraschino cherry.

Cherry Tree

Fresh maraschino cherries shaken with Skyy
vodka and cherry liqueur.

Chesapeake Martini

2 oz. Stoli Peppar vodka
1 tbsp. clam or oyster liquid
2 dashes hot sauce
1/2 tsp. Old Bay seasoning
1 cherry tomato
1 fresh oyster

Harbor Court
Baltimore, MD

Chesterfield

Belvedere vodka
Cointreau
juice of 1/2 fresh orange
juice of 1/4 fresh lemon
dash Martini & Rossi extra dry vermouth
sour mix
pinch of sugar

Place 1-2 drops of Martini & Rossi extra dry
vermouth in an iced cup. Fill with ice. Add
vodka. Add splash of Cointreau and pinch of
sugar. Squeeze orange juice in and drop the
orange (including rind) into the mix. Add
splash of sour mix. Shake until cold. Strain
into chilled glass. Garnish with a twist. For
sweet occasions, sugar the rim of the martini
glass.

Lola's
Chicago, IL

Chicago Lake Breeze Martini

1 1/2 oz. Stoli Persik
splash 7-Up
splash cranberry juice

Garnish with a lemon twist.

Chicago Martini

2 oz. dry gin
1/2 oz. scotch
green olive

Chili Pepper Martini

scoop ice
1 1/4 oz. Skyy vodka
1/4 oz. Goldschlager

Shake well, strain into cold martini glass.

Chilly Willy

1 shot Rumple Minze
1 shot Stolichnaya

Fill shaker to top with ice. Chill a martini
glass. Shake and strain.

China Blue Martini

gin
Canton ginger liqueur
blue curacao

Finished with large hunk of crystallized ginger.

The Martini Club
Atlanta, GA

Chinese Skyy Line Martini

Skyy vodka with chilled sake (floater)

Serve straight up in an oversized, chilled stem. Shaken, not stirred.

Skyy Martini List

Chinook Martini

2 oz. infused Smirnoff vodka
dash lime cordial

Infuse Smirnoff vodka with 2 parts fresh raspberries and 1 part fresh blueberries. Chill, strain, and top with fresh berries.

Chocatini

1 1/4 oz. Grey Goose vodka
1/2 oz. white crème de cacao

Sid Maples
Julie's Supper Club, San Francisco, CA

Chocolate Choo Choo Martini

Absolut vodka
Godiva chocolate liqueur
Kahlúa

Garnish with a chocolate kiss.

Chocolate Covered Cherry Martini

1 3/4 oz. vodka
1/4 oz. white crème de cacao
splash of Grand Marnier

Shake and strain into chilled martini glass.
Garnish with a maraschino cherry.

Chocolate Covered Raspberry

2 oz. Stoli Razberi
1 oz. Godet white chocolate liqueur

Chocolate Ghost Martini

1 oz. Stoli vodka
1/2 oz. white crème de cacao

Fill glass shaker halfway with ice. Stir and
strain into chilled martini glass, then chill 1/2
oz. Godet white chocolate liqueur. Strain and
float the Godet.

Toby Ellis
T.G.I. Friday's, Chevy Chase, MD

Chocolate Hazelnut

Skyy vodka shaken with crème de cacao and
Frangelico.

Lot 61
New York, NY

Chocolate Martini

1 oz. Absolut vodka
Godiva chocolate liqueur

Shake over ice. Strain into a chilled glass with a lemon twist garnish.

Chocolate Peppermint Martini

2 oz. Grey Goose vodka
1 oz. chocolate liqueur
splash peppermint schnapps

Stir and garnish with peppermint stick.

Chocolate Raspberry Martini

Belvedere vodka
white chocolate liqueur
dark chocolate liqueur
Martini & Rossi Rosso vermouth
raspberry liqueur

Garnish with fresh raspberry marinated in vodka.

Chocolatini

1 1/2 oz. Godiva dark chocolate liqueur
1 oz. Stoli Vanil vodka

Shake and strain into a chilled martini glass.
Garnish with a Hershey's Kiss, chocolate dipped
cherries, or a marshmallow.

Choco-Raspberry Martini

3 oz. Stoli Vanil
3 oz. Stoli Razberi
1 oz. crème de cacao

Shake and strain into chilled martini glass.

Chocotini I

2 oz. Stoli Ohranj
1/4 oz. Godiva chocolate liqueur

Serve straight up or on rocks. Garnish with an
orange slice.

Jill Stevens
Trabuco Canyon, CA

Chocotini II

2 oz. iced vodka
1/2 oz. chilled espresso
splash dark crème de cacao

Garnish with 3 espresso beans and chocolate shavings.

Chopin's #8

1 1/2 oz. Chopin vodka
1/4 oz. Chambord

Shake vigorously. Strain and pour into frozen cocktail glass. Float 1/4 oz. cranberry juice. Garnish with fresh raspberry (let it sink to the bottom).

Julie Grant
Puzzles, Atlanta, GA

Cinnamon and Spice

2 oz. Bacardi spiced rum
1/8 oz. Martini & Rossi Rosso vermouth

Garnish with two cinnamon sticks. Shaken, not stirred.

Red Head's
Chicago, IL

Cinnamon Martini

2 oz. vodka
1/2 tsp. Goldschlager

Mix vodka and Goldschlager with cracked
ice. Shake and strain into chilled martini
glass. Garnish with cinnamon stick and 3 Red
Hots.

Todd Greeno
Email

Cinnamon Martini II

3 1/2 oz. Smirnoff vodka
dash cinnamon schnapps

Chill, strain, and garnish with a cinnamon
stick.

Cinnamon Toast Martini

2 oz. Absolut vodka
1/4 oz. cinnamon schnapps
1 cinnamon wafer

Line the glass with cinnamon schnapps and
pour out excess. Pour the frozen Absolut
vodka. Stir with wafer and serve.

Jeremy Goring
The Observatory Hotel, Sydney, Australia

Cinnamon Toast II

1 1/4 oz. Stoli Zinamon
1/4 oz. Buttershots schnapps

Top with 1 spoonful or packet of sugar.
Sprinkle with cinnamon.

Andrew Holmes, Jardines
Kansas City, MO

Citron Martini

1 1/4 oz. Absolut Citron vodka
dash extra dry vermouth

Pour Citron and vermouth over ice. Shake or
stir well. Strain and serve in a cocktail glass
straight up or over ice. Garnish with a twist or
an olive.

Citron Martini II

Absolut Citron vodka
Chambord

Portland's Best
Portland, OR

Citron My Face

1 1/2 oz. Absolut Citron
splash Rose's lime juice
3/4 oz. cranberry juice
3/4 oz. pineapple juice

Shake vigorously so crystals appear. Strain
and serve.

Greg Chandler
Email

Citronini

Absolut Citron complemented with lemon
juice and sour mix.

Serve in sugar-rimmed martini glass.

Hurricane Restaurant
Passagrille, FL

Citrus Martini

3 oz. Stoli Limonnaya
3/4 oz. Cointreau
1/4 oz. lemon juice

Pravda
New York, NY

Citrus-Tini

2 oz. Absolut Citron
1/4 oz. Grand Marnier
dash Rose's lime juice

Garnish with twist of lime or lemon.

Brian Misenheimer
Houlihan's, Greensboro, NC

Claridge Martini

1 oz. gin
1 oz. dry vermouth
1/2 oz. apricot brandy
1/2 oz. triple sec or Cointreau

Shake with ice. Strain into chilled glass.

Classic Dry

2 1/2 oz. Bombay gin
splash vermouth
lemon twist

The Martini Club
Atlanta, GA

Classic Fintini

Finlandia vodka, chilled
garnish optional

Finlandia Fashion Martinis

Classic Olive Martini

Ketel One vodka
1 drop each dry vermouth and olive juice

Chill until bone-rattling cold. Strain into glass.
Garnish with 3 super-colossal Sicilian olives.

Jeff Nace
Olives, Boston, MA

Classic Vodka

Stolichnaya vodka, chilled

Garnish with lemon twist.

Renaissance Atlanta Hotel
Atlanta, GA

Cleanhead

1 1/2 oz. Stolichnaya vodka over ice

Top with tonic and two lime segments.
Squeeze limes well.

Clementini

fresh clementine

Shake with Stoli Ohranj and Grand Marnier.

Lot 61
New York, NY

Cloudy Day Martini

Absolut vodka
splash Opal Nera

Garnish with espresso bean.

Cloudy Skies Martini

Skyy vodka
splash sambuca
lemon twist

The Windsock Bar & Grill
San Diego, CA

Clove Martini

Freshly ground cloves shaken with Belvedere vodka.

Lot 61
New York, NY

Club Cocktail Martini

1 1/2 oz. dry gin
3/4 oz. sweet vermouth
1/4 oz. Yellow Chartreuse

Garnish with a maraschino cherry or green olive.

Club Lady's Famous In & Out Martini

"Always chill before you fill."

Chill 4 to 6 ounce martini glass.
Put in a dash of Martini & Rossi extra dry vermouth and then throw out, thus the name "In and Out."

Add Belvedere vodka to a shaker filled with ice.

Shake forcefully for about 30 seconds. Strain into martini glass. Garnish with 2 to 3 Club Lucky exclusive bleu cheese stuffed spanish olives and a lemon twist.

Club Lady
Chicago, IL

Club Macanudo

2 oz. Grey Goose vodka
1/2 oz. Lillet (French wine)
splash Grand Marnier

Shake, strain, top off with 1/2 oz. champagne.

Fernanco Aluardo
Club Macanudo, Chicago, IL

Cobalt Blue Martini

2 oz. gin
1/8 oz. blue curacao

Garnish with lemon twist.

Cocoa-Banana Martini

1 oz. vodka
1/2 oz. dark crème de cacao
1/2 oz. banana liqueur

Rim the martini glass with cocoa powder.

Code Red Martini

Skyy vodka
Grand Marnier
splash cranberry
twist

Coffee Martini

2 oz. Stoli Kafya
1/8 oz. splash Disaronno amaretto
1/8 oz. splash sweet vermouth

Cointini

2 oz. Stoli Ohranj
1/8 oz. Cointreau liqueur

Brasserie Jo Martini's
Chicago, IL

Cointreau Martini

2 oz. Finlandia vodka
1/8 oz. Cointreau

Portland's Best
Portland, OR

Cold Deck Martini

1 1/2 oz. brandy
3/4 oz. sweet vermouth
1 1/2 tsp. crème de menthe

Shake ingredients with ice. Strain into chilled glass.

Comfortable Possession

1/2 oz. Absolut Citron
1/2 oz. Southern Comfort
lemon twist

Shaken, not stirred.

Contemporary Martini

2 oz. Absolut Citron vodka
4 drops Cointreau

Fill shaker with ice. Add vodka and Cointreau.
Shake until well chilled and strain into martini
glass. Garnish with an orange peel.

Top of the Hub
Boston, MA

Continental Martini

Stolichnaya vodka
a ghost of dry vermouth

Garnish with a lemon stuffed olive.

The Continental Café
Philadelphia, PA

Cooperstown Martini

1 oz. dry gin
1/4 oz. French vermouth
1/4 oz. Italian vermouth
dash orange bitters
dash Angostura

Stir with a sprig of mint and garnish with a twist of lemon.

Copenhagen Martini

1 oz. dry gin
1 oz. aquavit
1/2 oz. dry vermouth
green olive

Copper Illusion Martini

1/4 oz. Cointreau
1/4 oz. Campari
1 orange twist for garnish

Serve in martini mixing glass filled with ice.

Michael Vezzoni
The Four Seasons Olympic Hotel, Seattle, WA

Coral Martini

Combine:
  2 oz. Smirnoff Citrus Twist vodka
  1/3 oz. freshly squeezed orange juice

Strain into martini glass. Top with chilled champagne. Garnish with orange wheel.

Coriander Martini

Freshly muddled coriander shaken with pepper and Skyy vodka.

Corkscrew Martini

1 1/2 oz. light rum
1/2 oz. dry vermouth
1/2 oz. peach-flavored liqueur or brandy
lime slice

Shake liquid ingredients with ice. Strain into chilled glass. Garnish with lime.

Cornet Martini

1 1/2 oz. Bombay gin
dash port wine

Stir in cocktail glass. Strain and serve straight up or on the rocks. Add lemon twist or olives.

Cosmo Kazi

1 oz. Stoli Limonnaya
1/2 oz. triple sec
1/2 oz. lime juice
1 oz. cranberry juice
1/2 oz. sweet and sour mix

Shake and strain.

Alan Hara
Club Miwa's

Cosmo Limon Martini

2 oz. Bacardi Limon
1/2 oz. Cointreau
1/4 oz. Rose's lime juice
3/4 oz. cranberry juice

Shake and strain into chilled martini glass.
Garnish with lemon twist.

Safari Lounge
Fort Lee, NJ

Cosmopolitan

1 1/2 oz. O.P. Anderson
1/2 oz. triple sec/Cointreau/Grand Marnier
1 oz. cranberry juice

Shake with ice. Serve on the rocks or in a
frosted martini glass.

Cosmopolitan Way Back When!

Cointreau
cranberry and lime juice

Garnished with an olive and orange twist.

Cosmopolitan Martini

2 oz. vodka
1 oz. Cointreau
squeeze 1/2 lime
splash cranberry juice

Shake with ice. Strain into chilled martini glass. Garnish with a twist.

Cosmopolitan Martini II

1/2 oz. Absolut Citron
1/2 oz. Cointreau
splash cranberry juice
splash Sprite

Strain over ice into martini stem glass. Garnish with barbed wire stirrer and lemon twist.

Brett Andress
Charlotte, NC

Cosmopolitan Martini III

vodka
blue curacao
cranberry juice

Garnish with a lemon twist.

Sheraton Seattle
Seattle, WA

Cosmopolitan IV

2 oz. Bombay Sapphire gin or Stoli Gold vodka
1 oz. cranberry juice
1/2 oz. orange liqueur
splash fresh lime juice

Garnish with a lemon twist.

Cosmopolitini

Absolut Citron
cranberry juice
Cointreau
Rose's lime juice

Polo Lounge
Windsor Court Hotel, New Orleans, LA

Cowboy Martini

Belvedere vodka
fresh mint leaves

Shake with sugar.

Lot 61
New York, NY

Coyote Martini

1 liter tequila
3 serrano chilies

Add chilies to tequila in the bottle; let sit for
48 hours or more at room temperature. Put
tequila in freezer until thoroughly chilled.
Serve straight from the freezer in chilled
glasses.

The Coyote Café
Santa Fe, NM

Cranberry Martini

1 part Godiva liqueur
1 part Absolut vodka
1 part cranberry juice

Combine with ice and shake well. Garnish
with a lime twist.

Cranberry Sauce Martini

1 oz. Gordon's orange vodka
1/4 oz. cranberry juice

Garnish with cranberries that have been
soaked in simple syrup.

Crantini

Finlandia cranberry vodka
Grand Marnier

Portland's Best
Portland, OR

Crantini II

2 oz. Bacardi Limon
touch Martini & Rossi extra dry vermouth
splash cranberry juice

Shake and serve straight up. Garnish with
cranberries and a lemon twist.

Crantini III

1 1/2 oz. Smirnoff vodka
1 1/2 oz. cranberry juice
splash lime cordial

Chill, strain, and garnish with a lime wedge.

Creme Brulee Martini

1 oz. Stoli Vanil vodka
1 oz. Kahlúa
3 oz. half and half

Shake and strain into chilled martini glass.
Garnish with light sprinkle of sweet ground
powdered cocoa.

Creole Martini

1 1/2 to 2 oz. vodka
dash dry vermouth, or to taste
large jalapeno pepper

Mix the vodka and vermouth in a shaker with
ice. Strain the drink into a chilled cocktail
glass. Garnish with pepper.

Crown Jewels

2 1/2 oz. Bombay Sapphire gin
1/2 oz. Chambord

Stir 50 times and strain into prechilled martini
glass. Garnish with large, fresh red raspberry.

Charlie Ryder, Beverage Director and Sommelier
LaSalle Grill, South Bend, IN

Csonka Martini

Absolut
Chambord

Garnish with Godiva raspberry chocolate.

Shulas No Name Lounge

Cub Campari

1 oz. Absolut Kurant
1 oz. Campari
1/2 oz. grapefruit juice
1/2 oz. cranberry juice

Serve in a martini glass.

Cucumber Martini

Freshly muddled cucumber shaken with
Belvedere vodka and lemon zest.

Lot 61
New York, NY

Cupid's Bow

1/4 oz. Cork dry gin
1/4 oz. Forbidden Fruit liqueur
1/4 oz. aurum (or curacao)
1/4 oz. passion fruit juice

Shake.

Curious George Martini

1 1/2 oz. Smirnoff vodka
splash banana liqueur
shot cranberry juice

Chill, strain, and garnish with a fresh banana wedge.

Czar

2 oz. Stoli vodka
1/2 oz. Chambord

Chill and strain into chilled martini glass. Serve with lemon twist.

Robert Gayle
Whispers Pub, Oviedo, FL

Czarina Martini

1 oz. Smirnoff Black vodka
splash dry vermouth
splash apricot brandy
dash bitters

Chill and strain into a martini glass.

Czar's Strawberry Cup Martini

Stoli Razberi
splash Godet white chocolate liqueur, chilled

Damn the Weather Martini

1 1/2 oz. gin
1/2 oz. sweet vermouth
1/2 oz. fresh orange juice
1 tsp. triple sec

Shake ingredients with ice. Strain into chilled glass.

Damn the Weather Martini II

2 oz. Finlandia vodka
1/3 oz. Veuve Clicquot champagne
1/4 oz. Chambord

Fill mixing glass with ice, add Finlandia and Chambord. Stir well and strain into martini glass. Top with Veuve Clicquot.

Windows on the World
New York, NY

Dark Chocolate Martini

2 oz. Smirnoff vodka
splash dark crème de cacao

Rub fresh mint leaf around the rim of the martini glass. Chill, strain, and garnish with a mint leaf.

Dark Crystal

2 1/2 oz. Stolichnaya Cristall vodka
splash Remy Martin VSOP

Stir with ice and strain. Garnish with lemon twist.

Compass Rose
San Francisco, CA

Dean Martini

2 oz. Ketel One vodka
chilled olive
1 Lucky cigarette and a book of matches

Pour the vodka into a cocktail glass and garnish with an olive. Place the cigarette and matches on the side.

Dean's Martini

Skyy vodka
splash Cointreau
cranberry juice
sweet and sour mix

Serve straight up in an oversized, chilled stem. Shaken, not stirred.

Decadent Martini

1 1/2 oz. Smirnoff vodka
float Disaronno amaretto
splash raspberry liqueur

Chill, strain, and garnish with a chocolate kiss.

Deep Sea Martini

1 1/2 oz. gin
1 oz. dry vermouth
dash orange bitters
1/4 oz. Pernod

Garnish with a twist of lemon peel.

Deitrich Martini

2 oz. Smirnoff vodka
splash Campari
splash dry vermouth

Strain and garnish with an orange peel.

Deliverance-Tini

Black Jack Daniel's
fresh lemon juice

Serve in a sugar-rimmed glass.

The Diner on Sycamore
Cincinnati, OH

Delmonico Martini

1 oz. dry gin
1/2 oz. dry vermouth
1/2 oz. sweet vermouth
1/2 oz. cognac
dash Angostura bitters
orange peel

Denise's Martini

1 oz. extra dry gin
1 tsp. extra dry vermouth
1 small drop red food dye

Shake with chipped ice. Strain into martini
glass. Add 1 extremely large green olive.
Dash of olive juice.

Denise Nalysnyk
Carpentersville, IL

Depth Charge Martini

1 1/4 oz. gin
1 1/4 oz. Lillet
1/4 oz. Pernod
orange peel

Derby Martini

Belvedere vodka
dry vermouth
1 olive

Serve straight up or on the rocks.

Hollywood Brown Derby
Walt Disney World, FL

Dernier Round Martini

1 1/2 oz. dry gin
1/2 oz. vermouth
1/4 oz. cognac
1/4 oz. Cointreau
dash Angostura bitters

Dewey Martini

1 1/2 oz. Absolut vodka
dash Martini & Rossi extra dry vermouth
dash orange bitters

Shake and strain into a cocktail glass or serve
over ice.

Diablo Martini

1 1/2 oz. white port
1 oz. dry vermouth
1/4 tsp. fresh lemon juice

Shake with ice. Strain into chilled glass.
Garnish with lemon twist.

Diamond Head Martini

1 1/2 oz. gin
1/2 oz. curacao or triple sec
2 oz. pineapple juice
1 tsp. sweet vermouth

Shake, strain, and serve with a pineapple
wedge.

Diamonds Are Forever

2 1/2 oz. Bombay Sapphire gin
splash scotch

Pour gin and scotch over ice and stir. Strain
into a well chilled martini glass. Garnish with
olives.

Gerard Lounge
The Sutton Place Hotel, Vancouver, BC

Diana Martini

1 1/2 oz. gin
3/4 oz. dry vermouth
1/4 oz. sweet vermouth
1/4 oz. Pernod

Garnish with a twist of lemon.

Dick St. Claire's

Ketel One vodka
cherry heering
freshly squeezed orange and lime juices

Diego Martini

2 oz. Smirnoff vodka
splash Jose Cuervo Gold tequila
dash orange juice

Chill, strain, and garnish with an orange
wheel.

Dillatini Martini

1 1/2 oz. Absolut vodka
dash Martini & Rossi extra dry vermouth
dilly bean (if you can find one)

Shake and strain or serve over ice.

Diplomat Martinit

1 1/2 oz. dry vermouth
1/2 oz. sweet vermouth
1/2 tsp. maraschino cherry juice
2 dashes Angostura bitters
lemon twist
maraschino cherry

Shake with ice and strain into chilled glass.
Garnish with lemon twist and maraschino
cherry.

Dirty Martini

1 1/2 oz. Bombay Sapphire gin
1 3/4 oz. extra dry vermouth
1 tsp. olive brine
stuffed green olive

Rub glass rim with lemon twist before pour-
ing. Garnish with olive.

Dirty Sicilian Martini

vodka
colossal Sicilian olives marinated in vermouth
    and some olive brine

Dixie Martini

2 oz. dry gin
1/4 oz. dry vermouth
1/4 oz. Pernod

Dog Bites Back

1 oz. Skyy vodka
1 1/2 oz. bloody mary mix

Stir with ice and strain into a chilled martini
glass. Garnish with olives and lemon twist.

The Martini Club
Atlanta, GA

Don Shula Martini

Belvedere vodka served straight up.

Garnish with cocktail mushrooms.

Shulas No Name Lounge

Dove Special

1 oz. Stoli Cristall
1 oz. Alize
1 orange twist

Matt Hoy
Sweetwaters Restaurant, Eau Claire, WI

Doyle's Dublin Martini (Boston Style)

1/2 oz. dry vermouth
2 1/2 oz. Jameson Irish whiskey

Pour into pint glass with ice cubes. Stir. Strain into chilled martini glass. 3 leprechaun size drops of Irish Mist. Slice from the rind of a lime as green as a field of shamrocks.

Eddie Doyle
Bull & Finch Pub, Boston, MA

Dr. Monahan

2 oz. dry gin
1/4 oz. Pernod
dash orange bitters
twist of lemon

Dragon's Breath

2 oz. Bombay Sapphire gin
splash vermouth
1/4 oz. Cointreau, flamed and poured into a glass
1/4 blood orange squeezed

Wedge of clementine as garnish.

900 West in the Hotel Vancouver
Vancouver, BC

Dressed To "K"ill

2 oz. Ketel One vodka
splash Grand Marnier
splash orange curacao and blue curacao

Pour into mixing glass, add ice, and shake
well. Add splash of soda. Garnish with orange
twist and maraschino cherry. Serve in chilled
martini glass.

Ric Storozuk
Northfield Ctr., OH

Driest Martini

1 oz. Absolut vodka
1 oz. Tangueray gin

Stir and pour into prechilled cocktail glass.
Add chunk of dry ice.

Brian Rea
Grass Valley, CA

Dry Gem

Bombay Sapphire gin
dash dry vermouth
black olive garnish

Renaissance Atlanta Hotel
Atlanta, GA

Dry Martini (5-1)

1 2/3 oz. gin
1/3 oz. dry vermouth

Stir vermouth and gin over ice cubes in mixing glass. Strain into cocktail glass. Serve with a twist of lemon peel or olive.

Dry Martini

2 oz. dry gin
splash dry vermouth

Shake or stir with ice and strain. Garnish with a green olive or twist. Serve straight up.

Dry Victoria Martini

3 oz. Bombay Sapphire gin
1 oz. Martini & Rossi extra dry vermouth
1 or 2 dashes orange bitters (or orange peel)

Garnish with 1 cocktail olive and twist of lemon. Shake or stir. Serve in classic martini glass.

Du Barry Cocktail Martini

1 1/2 oz. dry gin
3/4 oz. dry vermouth
1/4 oz. Pernod
dash Angostura bitters

Garnish with an orange slice.

Dubonnet Cocktail Martini

1 oz. Dubonnet Rouge
3/4 oz. gin
dash orange bitters
lemon twist

Stir with ice and strain into chilled glass. Drop in lemon twist.

Dutch Ketel

Ketel One vodka
Tomolives

Morton's of Chicago
Washington, DC

Dusty Martini

2 oz. Smirnoff vodka, chilled

Pour several drops of J&B scotch into the bottom of a martini glass, stir to coat. Shake out extra scotch from the glass. Strain vodka into the martini glass. Garnish with an olive.

Dutch Chocolate Martini

2 oz. Leyden gin
1 1/2 oz. crème de cacao
1/2 oz. lemon juice
1/2 tsp. grenadine

Shake with ice and strain into cocktail glass.

Joe Nacci, Beverage Manager/Bartender
Gibson's Restaurant, Chicago, IL

Easy Like Sunday Morning

1 1/2 oz. Grey Goose vodka
1 oz. Cointreau
1/2 oz. passion fruit sorbet

Shake and float champagne on top. Serve
with Chambord on rim of glass.

Robert Crane and Pamela Friedman
Mistral, Boston, MA

Eden Martini

1 1/2 oz. Smirnoff vodka
splash apple liqueur

Strain and garnish with fresh apple wedge
and a cinnamon stick.

Egyptian Club Chocolate Martini

1 oz. Absolut vodka
1 oz. Truffles dark chocolate liqueur
1/2 oz. Baileys Irish Cream

Mix ingredients into shaker with ice. Shake and strain into chilled martini glass. Garnish with chocolate covered maraschino cherry.

Kimberly Davis
The Egyptian Club, Portland, OR

El Martini Patron

Patron Anejo served in chilled martini glass. Hint of triple sec and lime.

Hurricane Restaurant
Passagrille, FL

El Presidente #1 Martini

1 1/2 oz. tequila
3/4 oz. dry vermouth
dash Angostura bitters

Stir ingredients with ice. Strain into chilled glass.

Electric Peach Martini

Finlandia vodka, chilled
1/4 oz. peach schnapps
1/2 oz. cranberry juice cocktail
1/4 oz. orange juice

Finlandia Vodka Americas, Inc.
New York, NY

Elegant Martini (Vodka)

1 1/2 oz. Absolut vodka
dash Martini & Rossi extra dry vermouth
1/4 oz. Grand Marnier
dash Grand Marnier

Stir the first three ingredients with ice. Serve on ice or straight up. Float Grand Marnier on top.

Emerald Martini

2 oz. Bacardi Limon
splash Martini & Rossi extra dry vermouth
splash Midori

Stir with ice. Serve on ice or straight up.

Enchanted Martini

1 oz. Encantado Mezcal
1/4 oz. dry vermouth
1 jalapeno or habanero-stuffed olive

Shake over ice in martini shaker. Strain into martini glass. Skewer olive on toothpick and add.

Mezcal Importers, Inc.
Napa, CA

Englewood Martini

1 oz. Stoli Ohranj
splash Campari
splash orange juice

Mix ingredients in shaker with ice. Pour into chilled martini glass.

Heather Puser
Hillsdale, NJ

Enos Martini

1 3/4 oz. dry gin
3/4 oz. dry vermouth
1/4 oz. Pernod

Garnish with a maraschino cherry.

Escobar Martini

1 3/4 oz. tequila
1/4 oz. dry vermouth

Garnish with a green olive.

Espionage Martini

1 1/2 oz. Smirnoff Citrus Twist vodka
splash white crème de menthe

Strain and garnish with a lemon twist.

Espresso Grande Martini

Finlandia vodka, chilled
1/2 oz. Kahlúa
1/4 oz. Grand Marnier

Finlandia Fashion Martinis

Espresso Martini

2 oz. Stoli Limonnaya
1/2 oz. Café Sport Borghetti espresso liqueur

Garnish with a lemon twist.

Espresso Martini II

Stolichnaya Kafya
splash Kahlúa and Tia Maria

Garnish with coffee beans.

John Dourney
The Thirsty Turtle, Basking Ridge, NJ

Exterminator Martini

2 oz. Smirnoff vodka
1/2 oz. fino sherry

Chill and strain into martini glass.

Fabulous Martini

2 oz. Smirnoff vodka

Chill and strain into well chilled martini glass.
Top with dash of champagne. Garnish with a
purple grape.

Fantasio Martini

1 1/2 oz. brandy
3/4 oz. dry vermouth
1 tsp. white crème de menthe
1 tsp. maraschino cherry juice

Shake ingredients with ice. Strain into chilled
glass.

Fare-Thee-Well Martini

1 1/2 oz. dry gin
1/2 oz. dry vermouth
1/4 oz. sweet vermouth
1/4 oz. orange curacao

Farmer's Cocktail Martini

1 1/2 oz. gin
3/4 oz. dry vermouth
3/4 oz. sweet vermouth
2 dashes Angostura bitters

Stir ingredients with ice. Strain into chilled glass.

Fascinator Martini

1 1/2 oz. Absolut vodka
dash Martini & Rossi extra dry vermouth
dash Pernod

Stir and serve straight up or over ice. Garnish with a mint sprig.

Faux Mint Julep

small bag of fresh mint sprigs

Throw them in the back of the fridge and forget them. Pour Maker's Mark over ice.

Drink, Happy Derby

Favorite Cocktail

3/4 oz. gin
3/4 oz. dry vermouth
3/4 oz. apricot brandy
1/4 tsp. fresh lemon juice

Shake ingredients with ice. Strain into chilled glass over ice cubes.

Feeney Martini

1 part Stoli Razberi
1 part Godiva chocolate (white or dark)
1 part crème de cacao (white or dark)

Shake and strain into chilled martini glass. Garnish with a strawberry or a chocolate kiss.

L'Opera
Long Beach, CA

Fernet Branca Cocktail Martini

1 1/2 oz. dry gin
1/4 oz. sweet vermouth
1/2 oz. Fernet Branca

Garnish with a maraschino cherry.

Ferrari Martini

2 oz. dry vermouth
1 oz. amaretto
lemon twist

Pour vermouth and amaretto into chilled glass
filled with ice cubes; stir well. Garnish with
lemon twist.

Fibber McGee Martini

2 oz. dry gin
1 oz. fresh grapefruit juice
1 oz. Rosso vermouth
3 dashes Angostura

Shake and strain.

Fifth Avenue Martini

1 1/2 oz. dry gin
1/2 oz. dry vermouth
1/2 oz. Fernet Branca

Fin de Siecle Cocktail Martini

1 1/2 oz. dry gin
3/4 oz. sweet vermouth
1/4 oz. Amer Picon
dash orange bitters

Final Approach

1 part Ron Rico rum
1 part vermouth
twist of lemon

The Windsock Bar & Grill
San Diego, CA

Fine and Dandy Martini

1 1/2 oz. gin
1/2 oz. triple sec or Cointreau
1/2 oz. fresh lemon juice
dash Angostura bitters
maraschino cherry

Finlandia Blue Moon

3 parts classic Finlandia vodka
3 parts pineapple juice
1 part blue curacao liqueur

Garnish with orange zest.

Finlandia Gold Digger Martini

5 parts classic Finlandia vodka
1 part pineapple juice
2 parts Cointreau

Finlandia Lime Green Martini

6 parts Finlandia vodka
1 part grapefruit juice
1 part Midori liqueur

Garnish with thinly sliced lemon and lime
twists.

Finlandia Midnight Sun Martini

5 parts Finlandia cranberry vodka
1 part classic Finlandia vodka
1 part Kahlúa

Finlandia Naked Glacier

7 parts classic Finlandia vodka
splash peppermint schnapps

Frost rim of martini glass with superfine
sugar.

Finlandia Pink Diamond Martini

3 parts Finlandia cranberry vodka
1 part pineapple juice
3 parts classic Finlandia vodka
1 part peach schnapps

Garnish with the perfect maraschino cherry.

Finlandia Topaz

5 parts classic Finlandia vodka
1 part dark crème de cacao
1 part Frangelico

Finlandia Buff

5 parts classic Finlandia vodka
1 part Baileys Irish Cream
1 part Kahlúa

Fino Martini

2 oz. dry gin
1/2 oz. fino sherry

Garnish with a green olive or a twist of lemon.

Fire Alarm Martini

4 oz. Absolut Peppar
2 oz. tequila
dash Tabasco

Mix all ingredients in shaker with ice. Pour
into chilled martini glass. Garnish with
jalepeno pepper.

Heather Puser
Smoke, Hillsdale, NJ

Fire and Ice Martini

2 oz. Smirnoff vodka,chilled

Shake in a shaker filled with ice and strain into
martini glass. Garnish with chili pepper.

Fire in the Hole

1 1/2 oz. Bacardi light rum
3/4 oz. peppermint schnapps
2–3 dashes of Tabasco

Firecracker Martini

1 1/2 oz. Captain Morgan rum
1/2 oz. grenadine
2/3 oz. 7-Up

Fill with orange juice, float Bacardi 151.

Firefly Martini

2 oz. Smirnoff vodka
3/4 oz. grapefruit juice
dash grenadine

Flamingo Martini

1 1/2 oz. gin
1/2 oz. apricot brandy
1/2 oz. fresh lime juice
1 tsp. grenadine

Shake ingredients with ice. Strain into chilled glass.

Flowers and Vines

3/4 oz. premium vodka
1 1/4 oz. Green Chartreuse

Dribble 3/4 oz. Chambord down side of glass to settle at bottom.

Rebecca Gass
Blueberry Hill, St. Louis, MO

Fluffy Duck Martini

1 1/2 oz. dry gin
1 1/2 oz. advocaat liqueur
1 oz. fresh orange juice
1/2 oz. Cointreau

Mix and top with soda water.

Flying Black Tie

3 oz. Grey Goose vodka
1/4 oz. scotch
1/4 oz. Campari

Stir and place into tumbler with ice, shake, and serve. Garnish with toothpick with a pearl onion in the center of two black olives.

Nelson Souza
Astor Hotel, Miami, FL

Flying Dutchman

1 3/4 oz. dry gin
1/4 oz. French vermouth
2 dashes orange curacao

Flying Dutchman II

2 oz. Beefeater gin
1/4 oz. blue curacao

Shake over ice and strain into chilled glass.

Foggi Day Martini

Beefeater gin
Pernod
dry vermouth

Mad 28
New York, NY

Fortunella Martini

1/4 oz. Campari
3/4 oz. Caravella
1/4 oz. Cointreau
3/4 oz. Bombay Sapphire gin
1 oz. Ketel One vodka
1 tsp. candied kumquat nectar
1 lemon slice

Coat ice cold mixing glass with Campari and
toss out excess. Add ingredients and ice,
shake, and strain into ice-cold martini glass.
Garnish with lemon twist and kumquat.

Four Seasons Olympic Hotel
Seattle, WA

Four Alarm Martini

4 oz. Absolut Peppar
2 oz. tequila
dash of Tabasco

Mix all ingredients in shaker with ice. Pour into chilled martini glass. Garnish with jalepeno pepper.

Heather Puser
Hillsdale, NJ

Fourth Degree Martini

3/4 oz. dry gin
3/4 oz. dry vermouth
3/4 oz. sweet vermouth
1/4 oz. Pernod

Stir gently with ice. Serve straight up or over ice. Garnish with lemon peel twist.

Framboise Martini

2 oz. Absolut vodka
1/4 oz. Chambord liqueur
1 raspberry

San Ysidro Ranch
Santa Barbara, CA

Frangelico Martini

1 1/4 oz. Absolut vodka
1/4 oz. Frangelico liqueur
1/2 oz. Tuaca liqueur

Stir with ice and strain into a chilled martini glass.

Pravda
New York, NY

Frank-A-Tini

Absolut Kurant
teeny-tiny touch of sweet vermouth and
    raspberries

No. 18
New York, NY

Freeborn Floater

Ketel One vodka
lime juice
Tomolives

Yvette Wintergarden
Chicago, IL

French Horn

2 1/2 oz. Absolut Kurant
1/2 oz. Chambord

Garnish with twist.

French Kiss Martini

2 oz. Stolichnaya Ohranj vodka
1/4 oz. Lillet

Stir gently with ice. Serve straight up or over ice.

French Martini

2 oz. Smirnoff vodka
splash cognac

Shake well and strain into a martini glass.

French Martini II
(aka Paisley Martini)

1/4 oz. scotch whiskey
1 1/2 oz. gin
lemon twist garnish

Froth Blower Cocktail Martini

2 oz. gin
1 egg white
1 tsp. grenadine

Blend and strain into chilled glass.

Fruit Burst Martini

1/2 oz. blue curacao
1/2 oz. vodka
1/2 oz. vermouth
1/2 oz. peach schnapps
pineapple juice

Place into shaker quarter filled with ice. Top with pineapple juice. Shake and serve in shot glass.

Kevin Hare,
Bedrocks Bar & Casino, Lower Hutt, New Zealand

Fruit of the Forest

fresh summer berries
Wyborowa lemon vodka

Garnish with berries.

Fruity Martini

1 1/4 oz. Gordon's grapefruit gin
1 1/4 oz. Stoli Ohranj vodka
1/2 oz. Chambord

Shake and strain into a chilled martini glass.

Fudgesicle Martini

Finlandia vodka, chilled
1/2 oz. crème de cacao
1/4 oz. chocolate syrup

Fuzzy Gator

2 oz. Stolichnaya vodka
splash peach schnapps
splash Gatorade

Garnish with a long lime twist.

Fuzzy Martini

1 1/2 oz. Smirnoff vodka
1/2 oz. peach schnapps

Chill, strain, and serve into a chilled martini glass.

Fuzzy Martini II

2 oz. Stoli Vanil vodka
1 oz. Stoli Persik vodka
splash peach schnapps

Garnish with thin peach slice.

Fuzzy Naval Martini

2 oz. Ketel One vodka
1/2 oz. peach schnapps
1/2 oz. freshly squeezed orange juice
orange peel for garnish

Ed Carlo
Bartender, Stage Left

Fuzzy Zinilla

3 oz. Stoli Vanil
1 oz. Stoli Zinamon
1/2 oz. peach schnapps
orange twist

Gilbert Valentine
Larkspur Restaurant & Grill, Wichita, KS

Garden Martini

2 oz. Smirnoff vodka
3 drops of dry vermouth

Shake and strain. Garnish with cherry tomato and pickled asparagus spear.

Gazette Martini

1 1/2 oz. brandy
3/4 oz. sweet vermouth
1 tsp. lemon juice
1/2 tsp. sugar

Shake with ice and strain into chilled glass.

Gene Tunney Martini

1 3/4 oz. dry gin
3/4 oz. dry vermouth
dash lemon juice
dash orange juice

Garnish with a maraschino cherry.

George's Way

Beefeater gin
dry vermouth
splash Pernod

Hamiltons
Miami, FL

Georgetown Martini

Ketel One vodka
splash Grand Marnier
orange slice

Morton's "Martini Club"

Georgia Peach

1 oz. Ketel One vodka
1/2 oz. peach schnapps
1 oz. orange juice

Stir with ice and strain into a chilled martini
glass. Garnish with peach slice.

The Martini Club
Atlanta, GA

Gibson Martini

2 1/2 oz. dry gin
splash French vermouth

Garnish with an onion.

Gilroy Martini

1 oz. gin
1 oz. cherry brandy
1/2 oz. dry vermouth
1/2 oz. fresh lemon juice
4 dashes orange bitters

Shake ingredients with ice. Strain into chilled glass.

Gimlet Martini

1 1/2 oz. Bombay gin
dash Rose's lime juice

Stir in cocktail glass. Strain and serve straight up or on the rocks. Garnish with lime.
                    OR
Shake, strain, and serve straight up or on the rocks with some ice.

Gin N' It Martini

1 1/2 oz. dry gin
1/2 oz. Italian vermouth

Garnish with a twist of lemon.

Gin Aloha Martini

1 1/2 oz. gin
1 1/2 oz. triple sec
1/2 oz. unsweetened pineapple juice
2 dashes orange bitters

Shake ingredients with ice. Strain into chilled glass.

Gin Cocktail

2 oz. gin
2 dashes orange bitters
lemon twist

Stir liquid ingredients with ice. Strain into chilled glass. Drop in lemon twist.

Gin Crusta Martini

2 oz. dry gin
1/2 oz. lemon juice
1/2 oz. Cointreau
tsp. maraschino
dash Angostura

Shake and strain into prepared glass.

Ginger Martini

Freshly muddled ginger shaken with a large
    pour of Skyy vodka.
orange zest
dash sugar

Gin Rush Martini

4 1/2 oz. Leyden gin
3 dashes Angostura bitters
1/2 oz. triple sec

Mix all ingredients with cracked ice in a shaker. Strain into chilled cocktail glass. Serve with lemon twist.

Joe Nacci, Beverage Manager/Bartender
Gibson's Restaurant, Chicago, IL

Ginsational Martini

1 1/2 oz. Schlichte Steinhaeger gin
1/4 oz. dry vermouth

Garnish with a twist of lemon and an olive.

Ginseng Martini

1 American ginseng root
1 bottle of vodka
Let stand for two days.

splash dry vermouth
ginger slice for garnish

Le Colonial
West Hollywood, CA

Gin Sidecar Martini

2 oz. dry gin
1 oz. lemon juice
1 oz. Cointreau

Shake and strain.

Gina's Chocolate Raspberry Martini

Belvedere vodka
white chocolate liqueur
dark chocolate liqueur
Martini & Rossi Rosso
raspberry liqueur

Garnish with a fresh raspberry marinated in vodka.

Rhumba
Chicago, IL

Gin-Cassis Martini

2 oz. dry gin
1 1/2 oz. creme de cassis
1 tsp. lemon juice

Shake and strain.

Ginka Martini

1 1/4 oz. dry gin
1 1/4 oz. vodka
1/2 oz. dry vermouth

Garnish with a lemon peel or a green olive.

Ginwin Martini

1 oz. Absolut Kurant
1 oz. Absolut Citron
1/4 oz. Grand Marnier

Garnish with twist.

Jason Bowers
Regas, Knoxville, TN

Glacier Blue Martini

Stolichnaya vodka
Bombay gin
blue curacao

Oliver's Mayflower Park Hotel
Seattle, WA

Glacier Mint Martini

2 oz. Smirnoff vodka
1/2 oz. peppermint schnapps

Strain into chilled martini glass.

Glamourous Martini

2 oz. Smirnoff vodka
dash orange juice
dash grapefruit juice
splash orange liqueur

Chill, strain, and garnish with an orange wheel.

Global Time

Tangueray gin
splash Chambord
lemon twist

The Windsock Bar & Grill
San Diego, CA

Gloom Chaser Martini

1 1/2 oz. dry gin
1/2 oz. French vermouth
2 dashes Pernod
2 dashes grenadine

Godiva Apricot Martini

1 part Godiva liqueur
1 part Absolut vodka
1 part apricot brandy

Combine with ice, shake well. Serve chilled
with maraschino cherry.

The House of Seagram
New York, NY

Godiva Black Currant Martini

1 oz. Godiva liqueur
1 oz. Seagram's gin
1/4 oz. creme de cassis
1/6 oz. lemon juice
1/6 oz. lime juice

Combine with ice; shake well. Serve chilled.
Garnish with maraschino cherry.

Godiva Cranberry Martini

1 part Godiva liqueur
1 part Absolut vodka
1 part cranberry juice

Combine with ice; shake well. Serve chilled.
Garnish with lime twist.

The House of Seagram
New York, NY

Godiva Mandarin Martini

1 part Godiva liqueur
1 part Absolut vodka
splash Cointreau or orange juice

Combine with ice; shake well. Serve chilled.
Garnish with orange slice.

Godiva Mint Martini

1 part Godiva liqueur
1 part Absolut vodka
splash white crème de menthe

Combine with ice; shake well. Serve chilled.
Garnish with mint leaf.

The House of Seagram
New York, NY

Godiva Naked Martini

1 part Godiva liqueur
1 part Absolut vodka

Combine with ice; shake well. Serve chilled.
Garnish with lemon peel or strawberry.

The House of Seagram
New York, NY

Godiva Nutty Martini

1 part Godiva liqueur
1 part Absolut vodka
splash Frangelico or amaretto liqueur

Combine with ice; shake well. Serve chilled.
Garnish with 3 almonds.

The House of Seagram
New York, NY

Godiva Raspberry Martini

1 part Godiva liqueur
1 part Absolut vodka
splash Chambord or raspberry liqueur

Combine with ice; shake well. Serve chilled.
Garnish with powdered sugar dripped glass
rim.

The House of Seagram
New York, NY

Godspeed Glenn Martini

3 oz. Bombay Sapphire gin
splash Noilly Prat vermouth
splash olive juice

Shake well with ice. Garnish with olive, twist
of lemon, and onion on a toothpick.

Renaissance Mayflower Hotel
Washington, DC

Gold Digger Martini

1 oz. Finlandia vodka
1/2 oz. Cointreau
1/2 oz. pineapple juice

Stir with ice; serve straight up or over ice.

Goldfinger

2 oz. Belvedere vodka
1/2 oz. Cointreau
1 orange slice
1/8 tsp. edible gold dust

Pour vodka and Cointreau over ice in a Boston shaker. Stir in gold dust and squeeze orange slice before adding to shaker. Shake and strain into a well-chilled martini glass. Garnish with orange peel.

Gerard Lounge
The Sutton Place Hotel, Vancouver, BC

Gold Martini

Stolichnaya vodka
Goldschlager
lemon twist

No. 18
New York, NY

Golden Girl Martini

1 3/4 oz. Beefeater gin
3/4 oz. dry sherry
dash of orange bitters
dash of Angostura bitters

Golden Goose

1 1/2 oz. Grey Goose vodka
1/2 oz. Grand Marnier
splash orange juice

Shake with ice vigorously to make ice crystals form. Strain and pour into frozen 'tini glass and serve with a "zest" orange.

Julie Grant
Puzzles, Atlanta, GA

Golden Martini

7 parts Gordon's gin
1 part French vermouth
twist of lemon peel

Golden Nugget Martini

2 oz. Smirnoff vodka
dash hazelnut liqueur

Chill, strain, and sprinkle with lightly roasted pine nuts.

Golf Martini

1 3/4 oz. dry gin
3/4 oz. dry vermouth
2 dashes Angostura bitters

Goose Berry

1 1/2 oz. Grey Goose vodka
1 oz. Godiva white chocolate liqueur
1/2 oz. Chambord

Shake with ice and strain into chilled martini glass. Garnish with 3 raspberries.

Jason Smith
Tavern on Rush, Chicago, IL

Goose Berry II

3 parts Grey Goose vodka
1 part triple sec
1 part peach schnapps
squeeze of fresh lime

Garnish with floating rose petals.

Brendan Card and Jose Carson
The Bubble Lounge, San Francisco, CA

Goose D'etat Martini

3 1/2 oz. Grey Goose vodka
3/4 oz. Lillet

Fill shaker with ice. Shake vigorously. Strain into chilled glass. Garnish with brie stuffed black olive.

Joseph E. Moorhead
Blackhawk Lodge, Chicago, IL

Goose the Monk Martini

3 oz. Grey Goose vodka
drop of Chartreuse

Shake over ice and strain. Set flame to it and serve with a twist.

Robert Sturdevant
Capital Grille, Boston, MA

Gordon's Continental Martini

Gordon's vodka
ghost of dry vermouth
lemon stuffed olive

Gordon's Cup Martini

2 oz. Gordon's dry gin
2 oz. port wine

Pour on the rocks in tall glass. Top with 7-Up or fizzy lemonade. Garnish with rounds of lemon and cucumber. Sprig of mint in season.

Gordon's Paradise Martini

2 parts Gordon's orange vodka
1 part orange juice

Shake with ice and pour into martini glass. Garnish with orange slice.

Gordon's Power Martini

1 1/2 oz. Gordon's orange vodka
1/2 oz. lemon juice
3 oz. orange juice
1 oz. raspberry syrup

Pour ingredients into mixing glass. Add ice, shake well, and strain into chilled martini glass. Garnish with orange peel.

Gotham

Smirnoff Black
dash Campari

Garnish with a trio of olives.

144

Gran Martini

1/3 shot Grand Marnier
3 1/2 oz. vodka

Fill mixing glass to top with ice. Strain into chilled martini glass. Garnish with lemon or orange twist.

Bob Phillips
Messina's @ the Crossroads, Email

Grand Crantini

2 oz. Finlandia Arctic cranberry vodka, chilled

Grand Martini

1 1/2 oz. Smirnoff vodka
splash orange liqueur
splash orange juice

Chill, strain, and garnish with an orange peel.

Grand Martini II

Stolichnaya Cristall vodka
light dash Grand Marnier

Garnish with orange twist.

Renaissance Atlanta Hotel
Atlanta, GA

Grand Obsession

Absolut Kurant
Grand Marnier
splash cranberry juice

Grand Vodka Martini

2 1/4 oz. Ketel One vodka
1/4 oz. Grand Marnier

Stir with ice and strain into a chilled martini glass.
Garnish with orange slice.

The Martini Club
Atlanta, GA

Granny Goose

Grey Goose vodka
splash Grand Marnier

Garnish with an orange twist.

Jim Jordan
Blue Light Café, San Francisco, CA

Grappa Martini

Stoli vodka
Grappa di Moscato

Garnish with olives.

Tunnel Bar Raphael
Providence, RI

Great Secret Martini

1 3/4 oz. dry gin
3/4 oz. Lillet
dash Angostura bitters

Garnish with an orange peel.

Green Hornet Martini

Finlandia vodka, chilled
1/4 oz. Midori
1/2 oz. sweet and sour mix

Green Lantern Martini

1/4 oz. Midori
1/4 oz. lime juice
1 1/2 oz. vodka
twist of lemon

Blend and stir.

Green Martini

1 1/4 oz. Stoli Ohranj
3 splashes extra dry vermouth
1/2 oz. Midori

Combine in shaker with ice. Shake well and strain into martini glass. Garnish with twist of lemon.

Jane Lomshek, Bartender
Holidome, Lawrence, KS

Green Room Martini

1 1/2 oz. dry vermouth
1/2 oz. brandy
2 drops Cointreau
orange twist

Shake liquid ingredients with ice. Strain into chilled glass. Drop in orange twist.

Greenbrier Martini

1 oz. dry gin
1/2 oz. Italian vermouth

Garnish with a sprig of mint and a lemon twist.

Grey Goose al'Orange Martini

4 oz. Grey Goose vodka
1 oz. Cointreau
splash Campari
splash peach schnapps

Flute
New York City

Grey Goose Passion

3 oz. Grey Goose vodka
dash dry vermouth
1/2 oz. fresh passion fruit puree

Combine ingredients in mixing glass. Stir gently. Strain into a chilled martini glass.

Albert Trummer
Danube Restaurant & Bar, New York, NY

Guards Martini

1 3/4 oz. dry gin
3/4 oz. sweet vermouth
1/4 oz. orange curacao

Garnish with an orange peel or a maraschino cherry.

Gumdrop Martini

2 oz. Bacardi Limon
1 oz. Belvedere vodka
1/2 oz. Southern Comfort
1/2 oz. sweet and sour mix
mist of Martini & Rossi extra dry vermouth

Sugar rim of martini glass. Shake vigorously.
Garnish with your choice of three tricolored
gumdrops, and a sugared lemon wheel.

Magnums
Chicago, IL

Gunga Din Martini

3 parts dry gin
1 part dry vermouth
juice of 1/4 orange

Shake with ice. Garnish with a pineapple slice.

Gypsy Cocktail Martini

1 1/2 oz. gin
1 oz. sweet vermouth
maraschino cherry

Stir liquid ingredients with ice. Strain into
chilled glass. Garnish with maraschino cherry.

Gypsy Martini

1 1/2 oz. Bombay gin
dash Martini & Rossi extra dry vermouth

Stir in cocktail glass. Strain and serve straight up or on the rocks. Add maraschino cherry.

H and H Martini

1 3/4 oz. dry gin
3/4 oz. Lillet
1/4 oz. orange curacao
orange peel

H.P.W. Martini

2 oz. dry gin
1/4 oz. French vermouth
1/4 oz. Italian vermouth
orange peel

Hakam Martini

1 1/4 oz. dry gin
1 1/4 oz. sweet vermouth
1/4 oz. orange curacao
dash orange bitters
maraschino cherry

Half & Half (French Kiss)

1 part Martini & Rossi sweet vermouth
1 part Martini & Rossi dry vermouth

Serve on the rocks and stir well. Garnish with
twist of orange or lemon.

Half & Half Martini

3 parts Bombay gin
3 parts Stolichnaya vodka
1 part dry vermouth

Garnish with lemon twist.

Hamlet's Martini

1 oz. iced vodka
1 oz. iced gin
splash dry vermouth

Garnish with cocktail onion on a sword.

Hanalei Blue Martini

pineapple infused Skyy vodka
blue curacao

Serve up in an oversized chilled stem.
Shaken, not stirred.

Skyy Martini List

152

Hanky Panky Martini

1 3/4 oz. dry gin
3/4 oz. sweet vermouth
1/4 oz. Fernet Branca
orange peel

Harikiditini

1 1/2 oz. shochu
splash dry sake

Shake and strain. Garnish with ume.

Alan Hara
Email

Harold's Martini

For those who never have more than one!

4 oz. dry gin
1/2 oz. French vermouth
dash orange bitters

Stir and pour into a 6 oz. carafe. Bury the carafe in shaved ice and serve with a frosted cocktail glass and a stuffed green olive.

John F. Bluhg
Email

Harry's Martini

1 3/4 oz. dry gin
3/4 oz. sweet vermouth
1/4 oz. Pernod

Stir gently with ice. Serve straight up or on ice. Garnish with mint sprigs.

Harry's Martini
(San Francisco Style)

2 oz. Bombay gin
1/4 oz. Green Chartreuse

Shake with ice and strain into chilled martini glass. Garnish with lemon twist.

Harry Denton's Starlight Room
San Francisco, CA

Hasty Cocktail

1 1/4 oz. dry gin
3/4 oz. dry vermouth
1/4 oz. grenadine
dash Pernod

Havana Club Martini

1 1/2 oz. light rum
1/2 oz. dry vermouth

Shake ingredients with crushed ice. Strain
into chilled glass.

Havana Martini

Ocumare white rum
dash mango passion

Hamiltons
Miami, FL

Hawaiian Cocktail Martini

2 oz. gin
1/2 oz. triple sec
1/2 oz. unsweetened pineapple juice

Shake ingredients with ice. Strain into chilled glass.

Hawaiian Martini

1 1/2 oz. gin
1/2 tsp. dry vermouth
1/2 tsp. sweet vermouth
1/2 tsp. pineapple juice

Mix all ingredients with cracked ice in blender. Strain into chilled cocktail glass.

Vania Thompson
Springfield, MO

Hazelnut Martini

Gordon's vodka
splash Frangelico
orange slice

Hennessy Martini

Hennessy VSOP
lemon juice

Shake and garnish with lemon.

Highland Fling Martini

2 oz. scotch
1 oz. sweet vermouth
2 to 4 dashes orange bitters
green olive

Shake liquid ingredients with ice. Strain into chilled glass. Drop in olive.

Hi-Life Camomile Martini

1 1/4 oz. camomile tea infused vodka
1/4 oz. honey

Garnish with lemon twist. Infuse vodka with fresh camomile for 24 hours. Take desired portion of vodka, shake, and strain into martini glass. Garnish with honey and lemon peel.

Michel Mourachian, Manager
Kevin Clayborn, Manager
Bill Kenny, GM
HI Life, New York, NY

Hilliard Martini

1 1/4 oz. dry gin
3/4 oz. sweet vermouth
dash Peychaud's bitters

Hillsboro Martini

1 3/4 oz. dry gin
3/4 oz. dry vermouth
dash orange bitters
dash Angostura bitters

Hoffman House Martini

3/4 oz. dry gin
3/4 oz. French vermouth
2 dashes orange bitters
green olive

Hole-in-One Martini

2 oz. scotch
3/4 oz. dry vermouth
1/4 tsp. fresh lemon juice
dash orange bitters

Shake ingredients with ice. Strain into chilled glass.

Homestead Martini

1 1/2 oz. Smirnoff Black vodka
dash Martini & Rossi extra dry vermouth
orange slice, muddled

Hong Kong Martini

2 parts dry gin
1 part French vermouth
1/4 tsp. sugar syrup
1 tsp. lime juice
dash Angostura bitters

Honolulu Hurricane Martini

4 parts dry gin
1 part French vermouth
1 part Italian vermouth
1 tsp. pineapple juice

Hop Scotch

2 oz. scotch
1/2 oz. dry vermouth

Float scotch on top.

Hot 'N Bothered Martini

DeKuyper's Peachtree schnapps
dash DeKuyper Hot Damn schnapps
splash vodka

Hot Lips Martini

Finlandia Arctic cranberry, chilled
1/4 oz. Goldschlager

Finlandia Fashion Martinis

Hot Potato

1 1/2 oz. Glacier vodka
dash of vermouth
dash Tabasco

Hot Spot Martini

Equal parts:
    DeKuyper Hot Damn schnapps
    Crantasia schnapps
    vodka

Hotel Plaza Martini

1 oz. dry gin
3/4 oz. French vermouth
3/4 oz. Italian vermouth

Fill a glass with ice; garnish with a pineapple
spear.

Hotzini

2 oz. Ketel One vodka
1 "Charleston Hots" pepper with pin holes
    (may substitute a serrano pepper)
1 fresh oyster on the half-shell
1/4 oz. Oscira caviar
1 frozen martini glass

Place 5 to 10 holes in pepper. Chill Ketel One
vodka in a shaker glass with a pepper. Pour
into frozen martini glass. Remove pepper
from shaker and put in martini glass. Present
glass on a small plate with oyster and caviar
atop as garnish.

Charleston Place
Charleston, SC

Hula-Hoop Martini

Finlandia vodka, chilled
1 oz. pineapple juice
1/2 oz. orange juice

The Finnish National Distillers Inc.
New York, NY

Iceberg Martini

2 oz. Beefeater gin
splash white crème de menthe

Stir with ice and strain. Garnish with mint.

Ideal Martini

1 1/2 oz. gin
1 oz. dry vermouth
1 tsp. unsweetened grapefruit juice
4 dashes maraschino cherry juice

Shake liquid ingredients with ice. Strain into chilled glass. Garnish with maraschino cherry.

Idonis Martini

2 oz. Smirnoff vodka
1/2 oz. apricot brandy
1 oz. pineapple juice

Chill, strain, and garnish with a pineapple slice.

Iguana

Absolut Citron
Midori
splash triple sec
twist

Imperial Cocktail Martini

1 1/2 oz. gin
1 1/2 oz. dry vermouth
1/2 oz. maraschino cherry juice
2 dashes Angostura bitters

Stir liquid ingredients with ice. Strain into chilled glass. Garnish with maraschino cherry.

"In and Out" Martini

2 oz. gin or vodka
1/4 oz. dry vermouth

Fill shaker glass with ice and add vermouth. Swirl ice around in glass and pour out. Add gin/vodka and shake vigorously. Pour into cocktail glass. Garnish with lemon twist or olive.

Patrick Ford
Smith & Wollensky's, New York, NY

Inca Martini

1 oz. gin
1/2 oz. dry vermouth
1/2 oz. sweet vermouth
1/2 oz. dry sherry
dash Angostura bitters
dash orgeat syrup

Stir ingredients with ice. Strain into chilled glass.

Indigo Blue Martini

Skyy vodka
blue curacao

Garnish with a lemon twist.

Bally's
Las Vegas, NV

Indispensable Martini

1 1/2 oz. dry gin
1/2 oz. French vermouth
1/2 oz. Italian vermouth
1/4 oz. Pernod

Inspiration

1 oz. Cork dry gin
1/4 oz. dry vermouth
1/4 oz. Calvados
1/4 oz. Grand Marnier

Mix and add maraschino cherry.

International Martini

4 parts dry gin
1 part French vermouth
1 part Italian vermouth
2 dashes crème de cassis

Irie Martini

Bacardi rum
splash Tia Maria
splash Grand Marnier

No. 18
New York, NY

Irish Martini

Tullamore Dew Irish whiskey
Baileys

Serve in cinnamon and sugar rimmed glass.

Cecilia's
Breckenridge, CO

Iron Curtain Killer Kamikaze

4 part Stoli vodka
2 part triple sec
2 lemon wedges
1 lime wedge
splash tonic
double splash 7-Up

Rob Styron
Scarcellas Italian Grille, Temecula, CA

Island Martini

2 oz. vodka (or gin)
1/4 oz. blue curacao

Garnish with orange speared with umbrella.

Jill Stevens
Trabuco Canyon, CA

Italian Ice Martini

2 oz. Smirnoff Citrus Twist vodka
splash sweet and sour

Pour into a glass with one ice cube and garnish
with a lemon twist.

Italian Martini

1 1/2 oz. Frïs vodka
dash of Hiram Walker amaretto

Italian Martini II

1 1/2 oz. Bombay gin
dash Hiram Walker amaretto

Stir in cocktail glass. Strain and serve straight
up or on the rocks. Add lemon twist or olive.

Italian Martini III

Belvedere vodka
Frangelico

Mad 28
New York, NY

Italian Martini IV

2 oz. Artic (Italian) vodka
1 oz. Campari

Italia-Tini

Stoli vodka
splash amaretto

Pazzaluna
Saint Paul, MN

Jack Frost Martini

2 oz. Smirnoff vodka
float peppermint schnapps

Chill, strain, and garnish with a peppermint
candy stick.

Jackie O Martini

1 1/2 oz. Smirnoff vodka
splash apricot brandy
dash grenadine
dash pineapple juice

Chill, strain, and garnish with a pineapple
wedge.

Jackson Martini

1 1/2 oz. Absolut vodka
dash Dubonnet
dash Angostura bitters

Stir with ice; serve with ice or strain.

Jamaican Martini

2 oz. Absolut vodka
1/2 oz. Tia Maria

Shake. Serve straight up or on the rocks.

James Bond Martini

3 parts Gordon's gin
1 part vodka
1/2 part Lillet

Shake ingredients with ice until very cold.
Pour into a chilled glass. Then add a large
thin slice of lemon peel.

Japanese Pear Martini

Fresh muddled pear shaken with Belvedere
vodka and zest.

Lot 61
New York, NY

Jazz Martini

Bombay Sapphire gin
lime juice
creme de cassis

Mad 28
New York, NY

Jeremiah Tower's Startini

2 oz. Belvedere vodka
2 drops Edmond Briottet Mandarin liqueur

Rinse glass with Martini & Rossi extra dry
vermouth. Stirred, not shaken. Garnish with
orange zest.

Star's
San Francisco, CA

Jersey Lightning Martini

2 oz. Lairds Applejack brandy
1 oz. sweet vermouth
3/4 oz. fresh lime juice

Shake. Strain into chilled glass.

Jet Lounge's Chocolate-Tini

1 1/2 oz. Ketel One vodka
1/2 oz. white crème de cacao
1/2 oz. Martini & Rossi extra dry vermouth
chocolate kiss

Reebok Sports Club

Jewel Cocktail Martini

1 oz. gin
1/2 oz. Green Chartreuse
1/4 oz. sweet vermouth
2 dashes orange bitters

Shake liquid ingredients with ice. Strain into
chilled glass. Garnish with maraschino cherry.

Jewel Martini

Bacardi Limon
Emerald–splash Midori
Sapphire–splash blue curacao
Ruby–splash cranberry juice

Gatsby
Boca Raton, FL

Jockey Club Martini

1 1/2 oz. gin
2 tsp. fresh lemon juice
1/4 tsp. white crème de cacao
dash Angostura bitters

Shake ingredients with ice. Strain into chilled glass.

Journalist Martini

1 1/2 oz. dry gin
1/4 oz. sweet vermouth
1/4 oz. dry vermouth
dash Angostura bitters
dash lemon juice
dash orange curacao

Joy Jumper Martini

1 1/2 oz. Smirnoff vodka
2 tsp. Kummel
splash lime juice
splash lemon juice
dash sugar

Chill, strain, and garnish with a lemon twist.

Judgette Cocktail Martini

1 oz. gin
3/4 oz. dry vermouth
3/4 oz. peach brandy
1 tsp. fresh lime juice

Shake liquid ingredients with ice. Strain into chilled glass. Garnish with maraschino cherry.

Jumpin' Jive Martini

1 1/2 oz. Smirnoff Citrus vodka
1 oz. pear liqueur
dash peach schnapps
splash cranberry and lime juice

Shake and strain. Garnish with pear slice.

Brendan Lee
Richards on Richards, Vancouver, BC

Jungle Martini

1 oz. dry gin
3/4 oz. sweet vermouth
3/4 oz. sherry
3/4 oz. pineapple juice

Jupiter Cocktail Martini

1 1/2 oz. gin
3/4 oz. dry vermouth
1 tsp. Parfait Amour or crème de violette
1 tsp. fresh orange juice

Shake ingredients with ice. Strain into chilled glass.

Just Peachy

1 oz. Stoli Persik vodka
splash Stoli Zinamon

Garnish with cinnamon stick.

Peggy Howell
Cotati Yacht Club & Saloon, Collati, CA

Kahlúa Dawn Martini

2 oz. dry gin
1 oz. Kahlúa
1/2 oz. lemon juice

Shake and strain. Serve with cocktail maraschino cherry.

Kangaroo Martini

1 3/4 oz. vodka
3/4 oz. dry vermouth
twist of lemon peel

Karamozov Koffee Martini

Stoli Kafya vodka straight up with a few coffee beans.

Kentucky Martini

1 1/2 oz. Maker's Mark bourbon
1/2 oz. amaretto
2 oz. Orange Slice soda

Stir with ice; strain.

Ketel Me Up Martini

Ketel One vodka
dry vermouth

Serve up with olive in chilled martini glass.

Hurricane Restaurant
Passagrille, FL

Ketel One Cosmopolitan Martini

Ketel One vodka, chilled
Cointreau
hint of cranberry

Division Sixteen
Boston, MA

Ketel Whistle Martini

Ketel One vodka
lime
cranberry juice
Cointreau

Ajax Lounge
New Mexico

Key West Martini

3 parts Malibu
1 part triple sec
3 splashes Rose's lime juice

Serve straight up in a martini glass.

Email
South Beach, FL

The Keywester Martini

1 oz. cream of coconut
2 1/2 oz. Bacardi light rum
3/4 oz. blue curacao
mist of Martini & Rossi extra dry vermouth

Garnish with a pineapple-stuffed cherry olive,
foil palm tree, sand, and blue water.

Keywester
Chicago, IL

Kiev Coffee Delight Martini

Stoli Kafya vodka
splash Stoli Zinamon and Stoli Vanil

King Eider

Mix 2 parts of your very best gin.
1 part King Eider vermouth

Garnish with a twist of lemon.

Duckhorn Vineyards
St. Helena, CA

Kiss in the Dark

Bacardi Limon
Martini & Rossi extra dry vermouth
cherry brandy

Stars
San Francisco, CA

Kiss Martini

1 1/2 oz. Smirnoff vodka
1/4 oz. Baileys Irish Cream

Dampen rim of martini glass and coat with
cinnamon-sugar mixture. Strain into a martini
glass and serve.

Kissin' in the Rain Martini

1 1/2 oz. Rain vodka
1/2 oz. Marie Brizard Parfait Amour liqueur

Chill and serve in a martini glass with lemon twist.

The Kiwi Martini

Fresh kiwifruit muddled and shaken with Ketel
One vodka and sugar.

Knickerbocker Martini

1 1/2 oz. dry gin
1 1/2 oz. French dry vermouth
2 dashes orange bitters

Stir with ice and strain into a chilled martini
glass. Garnish with lemon peel.

The Rainbow Room
New York, NY

Knickerbocker Martini II

1 1/2 oz. Smirnoff vodka
splash white crème de cacao
dash melon liqueur

Chill, strain, and garnish with honeydew melon.

Kremlin Martini

2 oz. Smirnoff vodka
1 1/2 oz. of crème de cacao
1 1/2 oz. half-and-half

Shake well. Strain into chilled martini glass.

Kris' Lime Martini

1 3/4 oz. Seagram's lime twisted gin
1/4 oz. Rose's lime juice

Garnish with a lime or lime twist.

K-Ting

Ketel One vodka
Ting (a grapefruit soda imported from
    Jamaica)

Nick and Eddie
New York, NY

Kurant Events Martini

1 oz. Absolut Kurant
1/2 oz. Grand Marnier
drop sweet vermouth
splash cranberry

Shaken and strained into chilled martini glass.
Garnish with raspberry.

Michael Golondrina
Orocco Super Club, San Francisco, CA

Kurant Martini

1 1/4 oz. Absolut Kurant vodka
dash extra dry vermouth

Pour Kurant and vermouth over ice. Shake or
stir well. Strain and serve in a cocktail glass.
Garnish with a twist or an olive.

L'orangerie Martini

ice-cold Tangueray Sterling vodka
splash Grand Marnier
orange twist

Oliver's Mayflower Park Hotel
Seattle, WA

Ladies' Choice Martini

1 1/2 oz. Absolut vodka
dash Martini & Rossi extra dry vermouth
1/4 oz. kummel

Stir with ice and strain.

Lady Godiva

2 oz. Smirnoff vodka
1/2 oz. Godiva chocolate liqueur
1/4 oz. white crème de cacao
cocoa
1 Hershey's Kiss

Landing Martini

Beefeater gin
splash Jose Cuervo Silver tequila
twist

The Windsock Bar & Grill
San Diego, CA

Last Round Martini

1 oz. dry gin
1 oz. dry vermouth
1/4 oz. brandy
1/4 oz. Pernod

Last Tango Martini

1 1/2 oz. dry gin
1 oz. orange juice
1/2 oz. dry vermouth
1/2 oz. red vermouth
1/2 oz. Cointreau

Shake and strain.

Lawyer Liberation Martini

3 parts Finlandia vodka
1 part Midori
3 parts pineapple juice
splash grapefruit juice

Laza Martini

3/4 oz. dry gin
3/4 oz. dry vermouth
3/4 oz. sweet vermouth

Shake with ice. Add slice of pineapple.

Le Ciel D'azur

2 oz. Skyy vodka
splash blue curacao

Brasserie Jo Martini's
Chicago, IL

Leap Year Martini

1 1/4 oz. dry gin
1/2 oz. orange-flavored gin
1/2 oz. sweet vermouth
1/4 oz. lemon juice

Lemon and Spice

Absolut Citron vodka
Absolut Peppar vodka
drop of dry vermouth
lemon twist

Cecilia's
Breckenridge, CO

Lemon Chiffon Martini

Finlandia vodka, chilled
1/4 oz. triple sec
1 oz. sweet and sour mix
squeeze and drop in fresh lemon wedge

Finlandia Fashion Martinis

Lemon Cosmopolitan Martini

2 oz. Absolut Citron vodka
1/2 oz. cranberry juice
splash triple sec
splash Sprite

Stir with ice and strain into a chilled martini
glass. Garnish with lemon twist.

The Martini Club
Atlanta, GA

Lemon Drop Martini

Absolut Citron and freshly squeezed lemon
with a sugar-rimmed glass.

Lemon Drop Martini II

Absolut Citron
splash lemonade

Serve in sugar-rimmed glass with a twist.

Cecilia's
Breckenridge, CO

Lemon Drop Martini III

Stolichnaya Limonnaya vodka
fresh lemon squeeze

Serve in a sugar-rimmed glass.

Lemon Drop Martini IV

sugar
1 1/2 oz. Absolut Citron vodka
1/4 oz. triple sec
1/4 oz. sweet and sour mix

Wet the rim of the chilled martini glass with
water. Dip in sugar and brush off any extra.
Stir the vodka, triple sec, and sweet and sour
mix with ice. Strain carefully into the sugar-
rimmed martini glass.

Tongue & Groove
Atlanta, GA

Lemon Grass Martini

Freshly muddled lemon grass shaken with
Belvedere vodka and lemon zest.

Lot 61
New York, NY

Lemonade Martini

Tangueray Sterling citrus vodka
lemon slice
sugar rind

Yvette Wintergarden
Chicago, IL

Lemontini Martini

2 oz. Stoli Limonnaya vodka
1/2 oz. dry vermouth
Cointreau

Line a cocktail glass with Cointreau and pour out excess. Combine vodka and vermouth over ice in a mixing glass. Strain into the cocktail glass.

Lenox Room Peachy Keen Martini

2 oz. vodka
1 tsp. peach puree
3 oz. peach nectar

Stir with ice and strain into a chilled martini glass. Garnish with peach slice.

The Lenox Room
New York, NY

Lew's Classic Martini

Beefeater gin
dry vermouth

Served chilled and straight up. Garnish with pimento stuffed olive.

Scott Hein, Bar Manager
South Lake Tahoe, CA

Liar's Martini

1 1/2 oz. dry gin
1/2 oz. dry vermouth
1/4 oz. orange curacao
1/4 oz. sweet vermouth

Stir gently with ice and strain.

Licia Albanese Martini

1 1/2 oz. dry gin
1/2 oz. Campari
twist of lemon peel

Serve over ice.

Lillet Cocktail Martini

1 1/2 oz. Lillet
1 oz. dry gin
twist of lemon peel

Lime Drop

Skyy vodka
lime juice
Cointreau

Shake and serve with a sugared rim.

Lot 61
New York, NY

Lime Light Martini

6 parts Finlandia vodka
1 part grapefruit juice
1 part Midori

Stir gently with ice and strain into chilled glass. Garnish with thinly sliced lemon and lime twists.

Limon Crantini

Bacardi Limon rum
cranberry juice cocktail

Martini's
New York, NY

Limon Martini

1 1/2 oz. Bacardi Limon
1/2 oz. Martini & Rossi extra dry vermouth
splash cranberry juice

Shake ingredients with ice and strain into a chilled martini glass. Garnish with a twist of lemon peel.

Limonnaya

2 1/4 oz. Stoli vodka
1/4 oz. sour mix
white sugar

Shake with ice; serve straight up or on the rocks.

The Martini Club
Atlanta, GA

Limon Twist

2 oz. Bacardi Limon
1/4 oz. Cointreau
1/8 oz. Martini & Rossi extra dry vermouth
wedge of fresh lemon

Limontini

Stolichnaya Limonnaya vodka
dry vermouth
Cointreau

Limontini II

1 1/2 oz. Glacier vodka
1/2 oz. Limoncello

Garnish with a lemon wedge.

Lindbergh Martini

1 part Absolut vodka
1 part peach schnapps
splash orange juice
orange peel

The Windsock Bar & Grill
San Diego, CA

Liquorice Martini

liquorice
dash sambuca shaken with Belvedere vodka

Lot 61
New York, NY

Lobotomy Martini

1 oz. amaretto
1/4 oz. Chambord
1/2 oz. pineapple juice

Chill.

Locomoko

1 oz. Stoli Ohranj
1/2 oz. triple sec
1/2 oz. lime juice
1 oz. cranberry juice
1/2 oz. orange curacao
1 oz. orange juice

Shake and strain over ice, blend or straight up.

Alan Hara, Club Miwa's

London Lemonade Martini

2 1/2 oz. Bombay Sapphire gin
1 oz. fresh lemon juice
1/2 oz. Rose's lime juice
1/2 oz. Cointreau

Garnish with lemon twist.

London Sun Martini

1 1/2 oz. Beefeater dry gin
1/2 oz. dry sherry
dash orange bitters

Garnish with a twist.

Lopez Martini

3/4 Absolut vodka
1/4 Disaronno amaretto

Combine in martini glass. Serve at room or chilled temperature, straight up. Garnish with slice of lemon.

Pio Lopex
Mom's Ristorante, Edison, NJ

Los Alto Martini

1–2 dashes Chardonnay
1 1/2 oz. El Tesoro Silver tequila
twist of lemon

Blend and stir.

The Love Martini

1 oz. Rain vodka, chilled
1/2 oz. white crème de cacao
1/4 oz. Chambord

Serve in chilled classic martini glass.

Lucky Mojo #99

Stoli Razberi flavored vodka
99 Bananas liqueur

Chill over ice and strain into a martini glass.

Louis Martini

1 1/2 oz. dry gin
1/2 oz. dry vermouth
1/4 oz. Grand Marnier
1/4 oz. Cointreau

Louisiana Rain Martini

2 parts Rain vodka
1 part vermouth
generous splash of Louisiana Gold red pepper
    sauce

Shake Rain vodka with vermouth and pepper
sauce in martini shaker over ice. Strain into
chilled martini glass. Garnish with red pepper
(optional).

Rain Vodka
New Orleans, LA

Loyal Martini

2 oz. Ketel One vodka
3 drops expensive Balsamic vinegar

Stir gently with ice; strain.

Lucien Gaudin Martini

1 oz. dry gin
1/2 oz. Cointreau
1/2 oz. Campari
1/2 oz. dry vermouth

Luxury Martini

Belvedere vodka shaken and served straight up.

Lychee Martini

Muddled lychees shaken with Belvedere vodka and lime.

Lot 61
New York, NY

Mad 28 Martini

Belvedere vodka
passion fruit
Hine cognac
cranberry juice

Mad 28
New York, NY

Madison Martini

2 1/4 oz. Bombay Sapphire gin
1/4 oz. Dewars scotch

Add ice to martini glass, fill with water. In ice
shaker add scotch, shake, and strain into
glass and drink.

Greg Hyde
The Ripple in Stillwater, Edna, NM

Madras Martini

1 1/2 oz. Stoli Ohranj vodka
1 1/2 oz. Finlandia cranberry vodka

Put in glass shaker filled half with ice. Stir and
strain into chilled martini glass. Garnish with
orange twist.

Toby Ellis
T.G.I. Friday's, Chevy Chase, MD

Mae West Martini

2 oz. Smirnoff vodka
dash melon liqueur
dash Disaronno amaretto
dash cranberry juice

Chill and strain into a chilled martini glass.

Magic Martini

1 oz. vodka
1/2 oz. Kahlúa
1/2 oz. Baileys Irish Cream
2 oz. milk

Shake into prechilled martini glass.

Pete Glavas, Bar Manager
Foghorns Bar n' Grill

Magnificent Seven (With Lemon)

2 1/4 oz. Ketel One vodka
splash Martini & Rossi extra dry vermouth
splash sweet and sour
splash cranberry
splash triple sec
sugar-rimmed glasses
fresh lemons
whole big dash of Love

Hi Ball Lounge
San Francisco, CA

Maiden's Prayer

1 oz. Cork dry gin
1/2 oz. Cointreau
1/4 oz. orange juice
1/4 oz. lemon juice

Shake.

Malacca Diva

Tangueray Malacca gin
dash triple sec

Hamiltons
Miami, FL

Malacca Martini

2 1/2 oz. Tangueray Malacca gin
splash dry vermouth to taste

Garnish with olive or twist of lemon.

Malibu Martini

Malibu rum
Bombay gin
dry vermouth

Garnish with a twist.

Malibu Rain Martini

Finlandia vodka, chilled
1 1/2 oz. pineapple juice
1/2 oz. Malibu
splash orange juice

Finlandia Fashion Martinis

Mandarin Martini

1 1/2 oz. Stolichnaya Cristall vodka
1 oz. Bombay Sapphire gin
1 dash Cointreau

Squeeze the juice of 1/4 of a mandarin orange
into the shaker (perfectionists should squeeze it
through a tea strainer). Garnish with mandarin
orange.

Mandarin Pencil Sharpener Martini

Bacardi spice rum
Martini & Rossi Rosso vermouth
splash sweet ginger syrup
fortify with gold flake and ginseng

Garnish with a candied kumquat incased in
pulled sugar.

Red Light
Chicago, IL

Mandarin Sunset

1 1/2 oz. Absolut Mandrin
1 1/2 oz. watermelon pucker
splash orange juice

Garnish with orange slice.

Mango 'Tini

fresh mango

Muddle and shake with Belvedere vodka and sugar.

Lot 61
New York, NY

Maple Leaf Martini

1/2 oz. amaretto
1/2 oz. banana liqueur
1/2 oz. cherry liqueur
1/2 oz. Midori
splash grenadine, cranberry juice

Shaken.

Pete Glavas, Bar Manager
Foghorns Bar n' Grill

Maraschino Martini

Bombay Sapphire gin
splash cherry brandy

Serve chilled and up. Garnish with maraschino cherry.

Scott Hein, Bar Manager
South Lake Tahoe, CA

Marcini

1 shot Absolut vodka
1 shot Cuervo tequila
extra, extra dry vermouth

Garnish with lime.

Marcie Jackel
Woodside Inn, Trenton, NJ

Mardi Gras Skyy Martini

2 oz. Skyy vodka
1/8 oz. blue curacao
1/2 oz. cranberry juice
fresh lime juice

Margit Martini

Bombay Sapphire
splash fresh lemon juice

Serve chilled and straight up with a lemon
twist.

Scott Hein, Bar Manager
South Lake Tahoe, CA

Mariners Martini

Line martini glass with Grand Marnier;
   swirl and dump.
Pour ice-cold Ketel One vodka into glass.

Garnish with orange twist.

Travis Krueger
Civic Pub, Coventry, CT

Marisa's "Outrageous Ohranj" Martini

1 3/4 oz. Stolichnaya Ohranj vodka
1/4 oz. Cointreau
2 drops Martini & Rossi sweet vermouth
orange peel

Chill over ice, slightly shake. Strain into frozen
martini glass.

Marisa Santacroce, Bar Manager
Santacroces' Italian Restaurant, Hood River, OR

Maritime Martini

1/2 oz. cherry-infused light rum
1 1/2 oz. pineapple-infused vodka
orange slice and maraschino cherry garnish

Blend and stir.

Maker's Mark Martini

2 oz. Maker's Mark
splash dry vermouth
twist

Martian Gibson

Grey Goose vodka
splash scotch

Garnish with an onion.

John Caine
Café Mars, San Francisco

Martinez Cocktail

dash of Boker's bitters
2 dashes maraschino
1 pony of Old Tom gin
1 wine glass of vermouth
2 small lumps of ice

*Jerry Thomas' Bar-tenders Guide 1887—Could
be the first martini.*

Martini Carib

1 1/4 oz. Cane Juice vodka
3/4 oz. Key Largo schnapps

Garnish with 3 grapes.

Stephen Dale
Bahama Breeze, Winter Park, FL

Martini "Manou"

Stoli Razberi vodka
Massenez Framboise

Martini au Chocolate

Godiva liqueur
Stoli Vanil vodka
dusting of cocoa

Brasserie Jo Martini's
Chicago, IL

Martini de Mure

Absolut Kurant
laced with creme de mure
    (blackberry liqueur)

Brasserie Jo Martini's
Chicago, IL

Martini for Two – 4.8 oz.

Ketel One vodka or Beefeater gin
dry vermouth

Serve with plethora of Tomolives, olives, and
cocktail onions.

Shulas No Name Lounge

Martini Jo

Stolichnaya vodka
whisper of Lillet Rouge and an orange twist

Brasserie Jo Martini's
Chicago, IL

Martini Melon

Finlandia vodka
soupçon of Midori and orange juice

Brasserie Jo Martini's
Chicago, IL

Martini Mint

2 oz. gin or vodka
1 oz. peppermint schnapps

Combine both ingredients in a mixing glass
with ice cubes. Stir and strain into a chilled
cocktail glass.

Martini Pernod

Beefeater gin
dash of pastis—the cocktail of Provence

Brasserie Jo Martini's
Chicago, IL

Martini Picante

Absolut Peppar vodka

Serve with jalapeno and olive.

Sheraton Seattle
Seattle, WA

Martini Refresher

1 1/2 oz. gin
1/2 oz. dry vermouth
1/2 oz. sweet vermouth
1 drop peppermint extract

Combine vermouth, gin, and peppermint over ice cubes in mixing glass. Strain into martini glass. Garnish with 1 or 2 mint leaves.

Judy Bernas
Tucson, AZ

Martini with a Kick

Absolut Peppar
hint of dry vermouth

Garnish with hot, red chili pepper-stuffed olives.

Shulas No Name Lounge

Maui Martini

2 oz. Smirnoff vodka
splash blue curacao
splash Grand Marnier
splash grapefruit juice

Garnish with a twist of lime.

Maurice Martini

2 parts dry gin
1 part French vermouth
1 part Italian vermouth
juice of 1/4 orange

Maxim Martini

2 parts dry gin
1 part Italian vermouth
2 dashes white crème de cacao

McKeegans Dream

1 1/2 oz. Bombay Sapphire (or Absolut)
1/4 oz. Bushmills

Shake and strain into martini glass.

Brett Egan, Director
National Bartenders School, Lakewood, CA

Mellow Yellow Martini

2 oz. Gilbey's gin
1 oz. Kina Lillet Blanc
1 drop Angostura bitters

Stir gently, don't shake. Serve in martini glass.

Melon Martini

Finlandia vodka
Midori

Garnish with a lemon twist.

Bally's
Las Vegas, NV

Melotini

1/2 oz. pineapple juice
1/3 oz. lemon juice
dash Angostura bitters
1/2 oz. Midori melon liqueur
1 oz. Martini & Rossi extra dry vermouth

Mix in stirring glass. Strain into an iced cocktail glass. Add a zest of lemon and spring mint.

Bogdan Dadynski
Trier, Germany

Menthe

1 oz. dry gin
1 oz. dry vermouth
1/4 oz. white crème de menthe
sprig of mint

Mermaid

1 oz. Stoli Ohranj vodka
1/4 oz. blue curacao
2 oz. pineapple juice

Shake in silver shaker. Garnish with pineapple chunk.

Maureen & Stephen Horn
Mermaid Martini Bar, Spiaggi, Cape May, NJ

Merry Martini

1/2 to 1 oz. dry vermouth
2 oz. Burnett's London dry gin

Shake well with ice, and strain into martini glass. Add olive or fresh cranberry.

Mervyn-Tini

Stolichnaya Pertsovka vodka
dry vermouth
caper berry

No. 18
New York, NY

Metropolis Martini

1 1/2 oz. vodka
1/2 oz. strawberry liqueur

Chill, strain, and top with 1 oz. champagne. Garnish with a strawberry.

Metropolis II

creme de framboise
raspberry eau de vie
Stoli Razberi topped with champagne

Lot 61
New York, NY

Metropolitan

2 oz. O.P. Anderson
1/4 oz. brandy
1/4 oz. sweet vermouth
1/2 tsp. simple syrup

Shake with ice. Strain or serve on the rocks.

Metropolitan Martini

Skyy vodka
strawberry liqueur
float champagne

Served straight up in an oversized, chilled
stem. Shaken, not stirred.

Skyy Martini List

Mexican Ice Cube

1 oz. Stoli Kafya vodka
1 oz. Kahlúa
4 scoops coffee ice cream
1 can mandarin oranges (strained)
4 oz. orange juice

Mix ingredients in blender until creamy. Pour
into shaker glass. Garnish with a slice.

Reid Jutras
Octane Inter Lounge, Rockford, IL

Mexican Martini

dash Jose Cuervo Gold tequila
top with 2 oz. Smirnoff vodka

Pour into a chilled martini glass. Garnish with
a jalapeno pepper.

Mexican Martini II

1 1/2 oz. Gran Centenario Plata tequila
1 tbsp. extra dry vermouth
2–3 drops vanilla extract

Shake and strain into an iced glass.

Miami Beach Martini

3/4 oz. scotch
3/4 oz. dry vermouth
3/4 oz. unsweetened grapefruit juice

Shake ingredients with ice. Strain into chilled
glass.

Miami Blue Moon

Skyy vodka
blue curacao
dash Grand Marnier

Hamiltons
Miami, FL

210

Michelangelo Martini

Combine:
 1 1/2 oz. Smirnoff vodka
 splash Campari
 1/3 oz. orange juice

Strain and serve with orange wedge.

Mickey Finn Martini

1 1/2 oz. Absolut vodka
dash Martini & Rossi extra dry vermouth
splash Hiram Walker white crème de menthe

Stir with ice and strain. Garnish with mint.

Midnight Martini

3/4 oz. dry gin
3/4 oz. sweet vermouth
3/4 oz. dry vermouth
1/4 oz. Pernod
dash orange juice

Midnight Martini II

1 1/2 oz. Smirnoff vodka
dash coffee liqueur
splash orange liqueur

Chill, strain, and garnish with an orange
wheel.

Midnight Martini III

1 1/2 oz. vodka
1/2 oz. Chambord

Stir with ice and strain. Garnish with lemon twist.

Gallery Lounge Sheraton
Seattle, WA

Midnite Martini

1 1/4 oz. Glacier vodka
3/4 oz. Echte Kroatzbeer Blackberry liqueur

Stir ingredients with ice. Strain into a chilled cocktail glass.

Midnight Sun Martini

5 parts Finlandia cranberry vodka
1 part Classic Finlandia vodka
1 part Kahlúa

Stir with ice and strain.

Milano Martini

Pour a dash of Campari and Cinzano into a chilled glass of gin.

Mile High Martini

1 part Stoli vodka
1 part Absolut vodka
1 part Skyy vodka

Shaken and stirred. Topped with an olive.

The Windsock Bar & Grill
San Diego, CA

Milky Way Martini

Ketel One vodka
dash Godiva and Baileys

Garnish with chocolate chips.

John Dourney
The Thirsty Turtle, Basking Ridge, NJ

Million Dollar Baby Martini

1 1/2 oz. gin
3/4 oz. sweet vermouth
3/4 oz. unsweetened pineapple juice
1 tsp. grenadine
1 egg white

Vigorously shake ingredients with cracked ice. Strain into chilled glass.

Minitini

2 parts Bombay gin
1 part white crème de menthe

The Windsock Bar & Grill
San Diego, CA

Mint Chocolate Kiss Martini

2 oz. Grey Goose vodka
1 oz. white crème de cacao
1/4 oz. green crème de menthe

Shake over ice and strain. Serve with a
chocolate stick.

Pete Savoie and Adryann Omar
Top of the Hub, Boston, MA

Mint Martini

1 part Godiva liqueur
1 part Absolut vodka
splash white crème de menthe

Combine with ice and shake well. Serve
straight up. Garnish with a mint leaf.

Mintini

1 3/4 oz. vodka
splash Grand Marnier
splash white crème de menthe

Chill and serve straight up in martini glass.
Garnish with maraschino cherry.

Mike Henry, Planet Hollywood
Atlantic City, NJ

Mistico Martini

1 oz. Jose Cuervo Mistico
1 oz. Chambord
1 oz. sweet and sour mix

Stir with ice and strain into a martini glass.

Mistletoe Martini

4 oz. Rain vodka
1/2 oz. Midori
dash grenadine

Mix vodka and Midori over ice. Stir and
strain. Add drop of grenadine which will
descend to the bottom of glass.

Rain Vodka
Frankfort, KY

Mobster

1 oz. vodka
1/2 oz. Jagermeister
add herbs

Mocha 'Tini

Freshly ground coffee beans shaken with Skyy
vodka and crème de cacao.

Lot 61
New York, NY

Mo Cocktail

Ketel One vodka
splash Chambord
5 squeezes of lemon juice

Chill until very cold. Serve straight up with a
twist.

Mo McLaughlin
Anchovies

Mochatini

1 1/2 oz. Bacardi light rum
1 1/2 oz. Bacardi spiced rum
1 oz. Oblio Caffe
dash Martini & Rossi extra dry vermouth

Shaw's Crab House
Chicago, IL

Modder Cocktail Martini

1 1/2 oz. dry gin
1/2 oz. dry vermouth
1/2 oz. Dubonnet
twist of lemon peel

Mojito Martini

juice of 1/2 lime
1 tsp. sugar
2 oz. white rum
soda water

Place lime juice and sugar in tall glass and
stir until sugar is dissolved. Rub mint leaves
around inside of glass and discard. Fill glass
with crushed ice, add rum, and stir. Top with
soda water. Garnish with sprig of mint.

Monealize

1/2 oz. Alize
1/2 oz. Southern Comfort
1 oz. pineapple juice
1 oz. orange juice

Highball glass, shaken, not stirred. Garnish
with orange and maraschino cherry.

Moneypenney

1 1/4 oz. Smirnoff vodka
splash raspberry liqueur
dash cranberry juice

Chill, strain, and garnish with a maraschino
cherry.

Monkey Bar's Banana Martini

2 1/2 oz. Skyy vodka
1/2 oz. creme de banana
1/2 oz. Martini & Rossi extra dry vermouth
caramelized banana

Reebok Sports Club

Monkey Business Martini

Finlandia Arctic cranberry vodka, chilled
1/4 oz. Malibu
1 oz. pineapple juice

Finlandia Vodka Americas, Inc.
New York, NY

Monkey Shine Martini

3 parts classic Finlandia vodka
splash peppermint schnapps
3 parts seltzer

Finlandia Martini Recipes

Montego Bay Martini

Malibu rum
triple sec
fresh lime juice
bar sugar—colored sugar-rimmed glass

Montgomery Martini

3 oz. Gordon's gin
1 tsp. plus a few drops Noilly Prat vermouth
1 olive

Montgomery Martini II

Tangueray gin, chilled until ice-cold
glance of vermouth

Garnish with olive, twist, or onion.

Renaissance Atlanta Hotel
Atlanta, GA

Montmartre Cocktail Martini

1 1/2 oz. gin
1/2 oz. sweet vermouth
1/2 oz. triple sec
maraschino cherry

Shake liquid ingredients with ice. Strain into
chilled glass. Garnish with maraschino cherry.

Montpelier Martini

1 1/4 oz. dry gin
3/4 oz. dry vermouth
cocktail onion

Moonshine Martini

1 3/4 oz. dry gin
1/2 oz. dry vermouth
1/4 oz. maraschino cherry juice
2 dashes Pernod

Morgan's Martini

1 1/2 oz. vodka
1/2 oz. Midori
touch of dry vermouth

Larry Clark
Morgans Tavern, Middletown, VA

Morning Glory Martini

1 1/2 oz. gin
1 oz. Stoli Vanil vodka
1/2 oz. Calvados

Garnish with cinnamon stick.

Chris Golz
Forbidden Fruit, Long Beach, CA

Mosquito Martini

1 1/2 oz. vodka
1/8 oz. Cointreau
2 drops Tabasco pepper sauce
squeeze lime wedge

Stir and strain into chilled martini glass.
Garnish with a sliced jalapeno.

Mother's Day Martini

3 oz. Grey Goose vodka
dash dry vermouth
dash rose water
3 fresh rose petals

Combine ingredients in a mixing glass. Stir
gently. Strain into a chilled martini glass.
Garnish with rose petals.

Albert Trummer
Danube Restaurant & Bar, New York, NY

Moulin Rouge Martini

1 1/2 oz. sloe gin
3/4 oz. sweet vermouth
3 dashes Angostura bitters

Stir and strain into chilled glass.

Moussellini Martini

Bombay Sapphire gin
splash Tuaca

Serve chilled and straight up with a twist of
lime.

Scott Hein, Bar Manager
LewMarNel's, South Lake Tahoe, CA

Mrs. Robinson Martini

1 1/2 oz. Smirnoff vodka
splash orange juice
splash Galliano

Chill, strain, and garnish with an orange
wedge.

Mud Puddle Martini

1 part Rain vodka, chilled
1 part Frangelico, chilled

Strain into a martini glass. Add dash of
Kahlúa.

Muddy Waters

Ketel One vodka
black sambuca

Yvette Wintergarden
Chicago, IL

Mumbo Martini

2 oz. Russian Roulette vodka
1/2 oz. olive juice
splash dry vermouth
3 cocktail onions
3 small onions

Mumbo Jumbo
Atlanta, GA

Muskovy Martini

1 oz. Stoli Zinamon vodka
1 oz. Stoli Ohranj vodka
1/2 oz. triple sec
1/2 oz. orange juice

Garnish with a pinch of cinnamon and orange
twist.

Muscovy Neapolitan

Equal parts:
    Stoli Razberi
    Vanil
    Kafya vodka

My Personal Martini

2 oz. Frïs vodka
1/2 oz. Glen Deveron 15 year single malt scotch

Serve straight up, very chilled, with a lemon twist.

Kasen Price
Email

My Secret Goddess of Love

2 oz. Stoli Razberi vodka
1/2 oz. Stoli Persik vodka
3 dashes grenadine
splash cranberry juice
splash pineapple juice
dash orange juice

Iris Vourlatos
Email

Myrna Loy Martini

2 oz. Smirnoff vodka
splash Lillet

Chill, strain, and garnish with an orange peel.

Mystique Martini

2 oz. Smirnoff vodka
dash Chartreuse

Chill, strain, and garnish with a lemon or lime twist.

Mysterious Jessy

1 oz. Stoli vodka
1/2 oz. Baileys
1/4 oz. Frangelico
1/4 oz. dark creme of cacao

Shake ingredients on ice and serve straight
up in martini glass. Garnish with cherries.

Alex Refojo
Club Mystique, Miami, FL

Naked Glacier Martini

7 parts classic Finlandia vodka
splash peppermint schnapps

Frost martini glass rim with superfine sugar.

Napoleon Martini

1/2 oz. Dubonnet Rouge
1/2 oz. Grand Marnier
1 1/2 oz. gin
twist of lemon

Blend and stir.

Naughty Martini

1 1/4 oz. Stoli Razberi
3/4 oz. Midori
cranberry juice
splash sour mix
float lemon wheel

Evan Horton
Pleasure Island Jazz Co., Kissimmee, FL

Negroni Martini

2 parts Martini & Rossi sweet vermouth
2 parts gin or vodka
1 part Campari

Pour over ice, stir well, and strain; garnish with a twist.

Nemo White Chocolate Martini

5 oz. Grey Goose vodka
2 oz. Godiva white chocolate liqueur

Pour both ingredients over ice into mixer. Shake 3–4 times, swirl, and pour. Rim glass with white chocolate.

Adrian Mishek
Nemo, Miami

Neon Martini

2 oz. Stoli Ohranj vodka
1/2 oz. blue curacao
1/2 oz. white crème de cacao

Garnish with orange twist.

New Yorker Martini

1 1/2 oz. dry vermouth
1/2 oz. dry gin
1/2 oz. dry sherry
dash Cointreau

Newbury Martini

1 oz. gin
1 oz. sweet vermouth
1/4 tsp. Cointreau
orange slice

Shake liquid ingredients with cracked ice.
Strain into chilled glass. Garnish with orange
slice.

Night Shift Martini

2 1/2 oz. Bombay Sapphire gin
splash Galliano

Stir with ice and strain into a chilled martini
glass. Garnish with olive.

Club 36
San Francisco, CA

Nightmare Martini

1 1/2 oz. gin
1/2 oz. Madeira
1/2 oz. cherry brandy
2 tsp. fresh orange juice

Shake ingredients with ice. Strain into chilled
glass.

Nineteenth Hole Martini

1 1/2 oz. dry gin
1/2 oz. dry vermouth
1/2 oz. sweet vermouth
dash Angostura

Stir and strain. Serve with black olive and flag.

Ninotchka Martini

1 1/2 oz. Smirnoff vodka
1/2 oz. white crème de cacao
splash lemon juice

Chill and strain into martini glass.

No. 5

1 oz. Ketel One vodka
1/2 oz. Bacardi Limon
1/2 oz. amaretto
1/2 oz. Tuaca
2 drops Martini & Rossi Asti dry vermouth

Garnish with rose petal.

Ralph Vega III
The Palace Nite Club, El Paso, TX

No. 18 Martini

Absolute Citron
Grand Marnier
orange slice

No. 18
New York, NY

230

Nome Martini

7 parts dry gin
1 part dry sherry
dash Chartreuse

Shake with ice. Serve straight up or on the rocks.

Number 3 Martini

1 3/4 oz. dry gin
1/2 oz. dry vermouth
1/4 oz. anisette
dash Angostura bitters

Number 6 Martini

1 3/4 oz. dry gin
1/2 oz. sweet vermouth
1/4 oz. orange curacao
twist of lemon peel
orange peel
maraschino cherry

Nuptial Bliss Martini

1 1/2 oz. dry vermouth
1/2 oz. Kirsch
1 oz. each of Cointreau, orange juice, lemon juice

Shake and strain.

Nut House Martini

Finlandia Arctic cranberry vodka, chilled
1/4 oz. amaretto

Finlandia Vodka Americas, Inc.
New York, NY

Nuttini Martini

2 oz. Smirnoff vodka
1/4 oz. Disaronno amaretto

Chill, strain, and garnish with an orange
wedge.

Nuttini Martini II

Stolichnaya vodka
touch of Frangelico hazelnut liqueur
orange twist

Cecilia's
Breckenridge, CO

Nutty Bacardi Spice Martini

2 1/2 oz. Bacardi spice rum
1/2 oz. hazelnut liqueur

Shake and strain over ice. Serve straight up.

Nutty Martini

1 part Godiva liqueur
1 part Absolut vodka
splash Frangelico or amaretto liqueur

Combine with ice, shake well. Serve chilled.
Garnish with three almonds.

Oahu Hurricane Martini

4 parts Gordon's gin
1 part French vermouth
1 part Italian vermouth
1 tsp. pineapple juice

Stir.

Ohranj Martini

1 1/2 oz. Stolichnaya Ohranj vodka
dash extra dry vermouth
splash triple sec
orange peel

Shake with ice and strain; serve up or on the rocks.

Old Estonian Martini

1 1/4 oz. dry gin
1 1/4 oz. Lillet
2 dashes orange bitters
2 dashes creme de noyaux
orange peel

Old-Fashioned Martini

2 oz. Smirnoff vodka
equal splash of sweet red vermouth and
    dry vermouth

Strain and garnish with a lemon twist.

Oliver Twist Martini

Dribble dry vermouth over ice in rocks glass.
Strain. Add Beefeater gin to top. No garnish.

Mr. G's Lounge
Deltona, FL

Oliver's Classic Martini

2 1/2 oz. Bombay Sapphire gin or
    Stolichnaya Cristall vodka
1/4 oz. Cinzano dry vermouth
2 large vermouth marinated Italian olives

Pour vermouth into empty martini mixing
glass. Swirl to coat inside of glass and dispose of excess. Fill coated glass with ice.
Pour gin or vodka over ice, shake vigorously,
and let stand 20 seconds. Garnish with olives
and strain mixture into glass over olives.

Oliver's
Mayflower Park Hotel, Seattle, WA

Oliver's Twist

Absolut Citron vodka
perfect twist of fresh lemon

Oliver's Mayflower Park Hotel
Seattle, WA

Olympic Gold

1 oz. Bombay Sapphire gin
1 1/2 oz. Absolut Citron vodka
1/3 oz. Canton ginger liqueur
1/6 oz. Martell Cordon Bleu cognac
1 lemon twist

Michael Vezzoni
The Four Seasons Olympic Hotel, Seattle, WA

Olympic Martini

1 3/4 oz. dry gin
1/2 oz. sweet vermouth
1/4 oz. Pernod

On the Runway

Stoli Ohranj vodka
splash Campari
splash orange juice twist

The Windsock Bar & Grill
San Diego, CA

On Time Martini

Bombay Sapphire gin
vermouth
olive

The Windsock Bar & Grill
San Diego, CA

One Exciting Night Martini

3/4 oz. dry gin
3/4 oz. dry vermouth
3/4 oz. sweet vermouth
1/4 oz. orange juice
twist of lemon peel

Coat the rim of the glass with sugar before
mixing.

One Martini, Straight Up with a Twist

Chill a martini glass with ice and vermouth.
Shake Ketel One in a shaker with ice until
frost forms on the outside. Dump ice and vermouth from the glass. Strain in vodka. Garnish
with a twist.

Opal

2 oz. O.P. Anderson
1/2 oz. white crème de menthe

Shake with ice. Serve straight up or on the rocks.

Opera Martini

1 1/2 oz. gin
1/2 oz. Dubonnet Rouge
1 tsp. maraschino cherry juice

Stir or shake with ice. Strain into chilled glass.

Orangeberry 'Tini

Fresh strawberries and orange shaken with Belvedere vodka.

Lot 61
New York, NY

Orange Boar

2 oz. Gordon's orange flavored gin
1/4 oz. Martini & Rossi sweet vermouth
splash Stoli Vanil vodka

Matt Hoy
Sweetwaters Restaurant, Eau Claire, WI

Orange Bowl

Tangueray gin or Gordon's orange vodka
vermouth
splash Grand Marnier

Garnish with orange slice.

Shulas No Name Lounge

Orange Delight

Stoli Ohranj vodka
splash dark crème de cacao

Garnish with fresh orange wedge.

Squirrel Morgan
Pier St. Pub, West Palm Beach, FL

Orange Delite II

1 oz. Stoli Ohranj vodka
3/4 oz. triple sec
1/2 oz. amaretto
2 oz. orange juice

Combine ingredients over ice. Top with
splash of soda water.

Lee Tepfer
Email

Orange Martini Kick

2 oz. Stoli Ohranj vodka in glass shaker with ice
1/2 oz. sambuca

Shake and strain into chilled martini glass.
Rub rind of orange on rim of glass.

Mike Polhamus
Bennigans, Fairfield, NJ

Orange Martini

1 1/2 oz. Gordon's orange vodka
1/4 oz. triple sec
1/4 oz. Martini & Rossi sweet vermouth

Shake with ice and strain into martini glass.
Garnish with orange twist.

Sam King
Bellingham, WA

Orange Martini II

1 1/2 oz. Gordon's orange vodka
dash extra dry vermouth
splash triple sec
orange peel

Shake with ice and strain. Serve straight up or
on the rocks.

Orange Martini III

2 oz. vodka
1 tsp. Grand Marnier
orange peel

Mix vodka and Grand Marnier with cracked
ice. Shake vigorously. Take chilled martini
glass and rub inside with orange peel. Shake
again and strain into martini glass. Garnish
with 3 dried cherries.

Todd Greeno
New York, NY

Orange Mochatini

2 oz. Stoli Kafya vodka
1 oz. Stoli Vanil vodka
splash chocolate liqueur
splash orange liqueur

Garnish with 3 coffee beans or orange twist.

Orange Truffle

Mix: orange-flavored vodka
     white-chocolate liqueur

The Velvet Lounge
Detroit, MI

Orangetini

1 1/2 oz. Absolut vodka
dash Martini & Rossi extra dry vermouth
splash Hiram Walker triple sec

Stir gently and strain over ice. Garnish with
an orange peel.

Ohranj You Special

1 oz. Stoli Ohranj vodka
splash Grand Marnier

Garnish with shaved orange peel.

Peggy Howell
Cotati Yacht Club & Saloon, Cotati, CA

Orchid Petal

1 1/2 oz. O.P. Anderson
1/2 oz. raspberry liqueur or Chambord

Shake with ice. Serve straight up or on the
rocks.

Original Martinez Cocktail

1 part Old Tom gin
1 part sweet vermouth
2 dashes simple syrup
dash maraschino juice
dash Angostura bitters
slice of lemon

Original Sin Martini

Equal parts:
    DeKuyper Apple Barrel schnapps
    vodka

Oyster Martini

Frosty Skyy vodka martini

Shake and pour over freshly shucked oyster from the raw bar.

Eastside West
San Francisco, CA

Ozzon Martini

2 1/2 oz. Skyy vodka
splash Romana sambuca
1 olive for garnish

Stir with ice and strain into a chilled martini glass. Garnish with olive.

Club 36
San Francisco, CA

Paisley

2 oz. Bombay Sapphire gin
1/2 oz. single malt scotch whiskey
1/2 oz. dry vermouth

Garnish with a twist.

Pall Mall Martini

1 1/2 oz. gin
1/2 oz. dry vermouth
1/2 oz. sweet vermouth
1 tsp. white crème de menthe
dash Angostura bitters, optional

Stir ingredients with ice.

Palmetto Martini

1 1/2 oz. rum
1 oz. sweet vermouth
2 dashes of bitters

Chill, strain, and serve in a chilled glass.
Garnish with a lemon twist.

Panache Martini

2 1/2 oz. Grey Goose vodka
1/4 oz. Pernod
1/4 oz. white crème de menthe
whisper of dry vermouth

Gary Marcarelli
Meridien Hotel, Boston, MA

Paradigm Shift

"Entering an alternative Martini dimension."

1/8 oz. Campari
1 oz. fresh squeezed Texas Ruby Red
     grapefruit juice
1 oz. fresh raspberry lemon-lime sour
2 oz. Rain vodka
3/4 oz. Bombay gin

Start with an empty ice-cold martini mixing
glass. Lightly coat the mixing glass with
Campari. Dispose of excess. Fill mixing glass
with ice. Squeeze Texas Ruby Red grapefruit
into glass. Add fresh raspberry lemon-lime
sour. Pour Rain vodka and Bombay gin into
mixing glass. Cap and shake vigorously. Strain
the mixture into frozen martini glass. Garnish
with frozen grapefruit slice and fresh frozen
raspberry.

Oliver's
Mayflower Park Hotel, Seattle, WA

Paris Carver Martini

2 oz. Smirnoff vodka
splash Romana Black sambuca

Run a lime wedge around the rim of a martini
glass and coat with sugar. Chill, strain, and
garnish with a lime.

Parisian Kiss Martini

2 oz. Smirnoff vodka
splash Pernod

Chill, strain, and sprinkle with juniper
berries.

Parisian Martini

1 oz. gin
1 oz. dry vermouth
1 oz. creme de cassis

Chill and strain into a chilled martini glass.

Parisian Martini II

2 1/2 oz. Tangueray gin
dash Pernod
1 Tomolive for garnish

Stir with ice and strain into a chilled martini
glass. Garnish with a Tomolive.

Compass Rose
San Francisco, CA

Park Avenue Martini

1 1/2 oz. gin
1/2 oz. sweet vermouth
1 oz. pineapple juice
2–3 drops of curacao

Chill and strain into a chilled martini glass.

Park Place Martini

1 oz. Bombay Sapphire gin
1 oz. Chambord
dash triple sec
lemon zest

Pasha Martini

2 oz. Grey Goose
1 oz. Midori

Shake rapidly over ice. Pour in 1/2–1 oz.
Chambord. No garnish.

Jim Bacus
Pasha, Chicago, IL

Parrot Head

Midori
Malibu
pineapple juice
grenadine

Gatsby
Boca Raton, FL

Passion Fruit Martini

vodka
Alize
hint Remy Martin
hint cranberry juice

Patsy's Martini

1 1/2 oz. Stoli vodka
1 oz. champagne

The Martini Club
Atlanta, GA

Peach Dream Martini

1 oz. Stoli Persik vodka
splash peach schnapps
splash Malibu rum

Serve on the rocks strained in a chilled "up" glass.

Eric Schmidt
Café Winberie, Oak Park, IL

Peaches & Cream

1 1/2 oz. Stoli Persik
1/2 oz. Stoli Vanil
1 peach slice as garnish

Club XIX at the Lodge at Pebble Beach
Pebble Beach, CA

Peach Fuzz

Stoli Persik vodka
peach schnapps
triple sec
splash orange juice

Gatsby
Boca Raton, FL

Peach Highrise Martini

2 oz. Stoli Persik vodka
splash cranberry juice
splash fresh lime juice
lime wedge

Peach Martini

Skyy vodka
peach schnapps

Portland's Best
Portland, OR

Peachie-Keen Martini

Finlandia Artic cranberry vodka, chilled
1/4 oz. peach schnapps

Finlandia Vodka Americas, Inc.
New York, NY

Pear Martini

2 oz. Grey Goose vodka
1/2 oz. Cointreau
1/2 oz. fresh squeezed lime juice

Rim glass with sugar and dried orange rind.

Thomas Mastricola
9 Park, Boston, MA

Pear Martini II

2 oz. Stolichnaya vodka
1/2 oz. Perle de Brillet liqueur

Garnish with pear slice.

Pear Martini III

Ketel One vodka

Flavor with dash of Perle de Brillet, a
pear/cognac liqueur, and a lemon twist.

Renaissance Atlanta Hotel
Atlanta, GA

Peatini

1 oz. gin
splash vermouth
1 Texas sized black-eyed pea

Shake with crushed ice, pour into glass.

Marianne Stevens
Email

Peggy Martini

1 1/2 oz. dry gin
3/4 oz. dry vermouth
1/4 oz. Pernod
1/4 oz. Dubonnet

250

Peppar Martini

Absolut Peppar vodka
Cinzano dry vermouth
jalapeno-stuffed olive

Peppermint Martini

2 oz. vodka
1/2 oz. Rumple Minze

Shake.

Peppermint Patty Martini

2 1/2 oz. Grey Goose vodka
1/2 oz. peppermint schnapps
1/2 oz. white crème de cacao

Garnish with two Junior Mints on a pick.

Michael Mika of Harvey's
Boston, MA

Peppertini

1 1/2 oz. Stoli Pertsovka vodka
1/2 oz. dry vermouth
olive garnish

Mix Pertsovka and dry vermouth in cocktail
shaker over ice, stir, and strain.

Perfect Martini

1 3/4 oz. gin
1/4 oz. sweet vermouth
1/4 oz. dry vermouth
twist of lemon

Blend and stir.

Perfect Martini II

2 oz. dry gin
1/4 oz. French vermouth
1/4 oz. Italian vermouth
dash bitters
twist of lemon peel

Perfect Martini III

4 oz. Bombay Sapphire gin
1 oz. each: French and Italian vermouth
dash orange bitters

Garnish with orange twist.

Adapted from Nassau Gun Club recipe

Perfect Pair

1 1/2 oz. Grey Goose vodka
1/2 oz. Pear eau de vie
1/2 oz. fresh lemon juice
1/2 oz. simple syrup
splash orange juice

Marco Dianysos
Absinthe, San Francisco, CA

Perfect Royal Martini

3/4 oz. dry gin
3/4 oz. dry vermouth
3/4 oz. sweet vermouth
1/4 oz. Pernod
green cherry

Perfection Martini

1 1/2 oz. Bombay gin
dash Martini & Rossi Rosso vermouth

Stir in cocktail glass. Strain and serve straight
up or on the rocks. Add lemon twist or olives.
                    OR
Shake, strain, and serve straight up or on the
rocks with some ice.

Perfection Martini II

1 3/4 oz. dry gin
1/2 oz. sweet vermouth
1/2 oz. orange juice

253

Pernod Martini

2 oz. dry gin
1/2 oz. dry vermouth
2 dashes Pernod

Phantom Martini

Ketel One vodka
splash Johnny Walker Black Label
jumbo black olive

Morton's "Martini Club"
San Antonio, TX

Piccadilly Cocktail Martini

1 1/2 oz. gin
3/4 oz. dry vermouth
1/4 tsp. Pernod or other anise-flavored liqueur
1/4 tsp. grenadine

Stir ingredients with ice. Strain into chilled glass.

Pickled Pepper Martini

2 oz. Absolut Peppar vodka
splash pickle juice

Shake and strain into chilled martini glass.
Garnish with thick slice of dill pickle.

Pomona, CA

Pinacranakaze Martini

pineapple infused Skyy vodka
lime and cranberry juice

Serve straight up in an oversized, chilled
stem. Shaken, not stirred.

Skyy Martini List

Pink Diamond Martini

1 part Finlandia cranberry vodka
3 parts classic Finlandia vodka
1 part peach schnapps
pineapple juice

Stir gently with ice and strain. Garnish with a
perfect maraschino cherry or rose petals
floated on top.

Pink Martini

1 1/2 oz. Absolut vodka
1/2 oz. cranberry juice
dash dry vermouth

Garnish with lime squeeze.

Randy Wickstrom
Rainforest, Beach Park, IL

Pink Martini Twist

Absolut Kurant vodka
Chambord

Portland's Best
Portland, OR

Pink Poodle Martini

3/4 oz. Stoli Cristall vodka
1/4 oz. white crème de cacao
1/4 oz. Chambord

Mix over ice and strain into chilled martini
glass. Garnish with fresh raspberry.

Scott DiStefano
Susie's Bar, Calistoga, CA

Pink Rose

Skyy vodka
DeKuyper Peachtree schnapps
dash cranberry juice

Hamiltons
Miami, FL

Pink Stingray Martini

Finlandia cranberry vodka
white crème de cacao

Portland's Best
Portland, OR

Pink Swan Cocktail

Bacardi Anejo rum
Cointreau
sweet and sour mix
2 maraschino cherries

Blend with ice. Rim martini glass with sugar.
Garnish with lime circle, maraschino cherry,
and short straws.

Hotel Bel-Air
Los Angeles, CA

Pinsk Peach

Stoli Persik vodka and Campari straight up.

Pitbull in the Sky

Skyy vodka
splash grapefruit juice and a twist

Serve straight up in an oversized chilled
stem. Shaken, not stirred.

Skyy Martini List

Pitbull Martini

Gordon's vodka
splash grapefruit juice
twist

Plaza Martini

1 1/2 oz. Bombay gin
1 1/2 oz. Martini & Rossi extra dry vermouth

Stir in cocktail glass. Strain and serve straight
up or on the rocks. Add lemon twist or olives.

Plaza Martini II

1 oz. dry gin
1 oz. dry vermouth
1 oz. sweet vermouth
splash pineapple juice

Plymouth Cocktail Martini

2 1/2 oz. dry gin
2 dashes orange bitters

Poet's Dream Martini

1 oz. dry gin
3/4 oz. dry vermouth
3/4 oz. Benedictine
twist of lemon peel

Poinsettia Martini

1 1/2 oz. Absolut vodka
1/4 oz. Chambord
1/4 oz. pineapple juice

Shake with ice and strain into martini glass.

Linda Bett
Longneckers Saloon, Houston, TX

Polo Cocktail Martini

1 1/2 oz. gin
3/4 oz. fresh orange juice
1/2 oz. fresh lemon juice

Shake ingredients with ice. Strain into chilled glass.

Polo Martini

1 1/2 oz. vodka
1 1/2 oz. Perrier-Jouet champagne
dash Peychaud bitters

Serve straight up in martini glass. Garnish with olive and twist on the side.

Windsor Court Hotel
New Orleans, LA

Polo Martini Club

1 oz. dry gin
1/2 oz. dry vermouth
1/3 oz. sweet vermouth
1/4 oz. lime juice

Polynesian Martini

1 1/2 oz. Smirnoff vodka
3/4 oz. cherry-flavored brandy
splash lime juice

Chill and strain into martini glass with powdered sugar rim.

Pom Pom Martini

1 1/2 oz. dry vermouth
3/4 oz. dry gin
2 dashes orange bitters

Pomegranate Martini

Stoli Razberi vodka shaken with pomegranate seed and lime.

Lot 61
New York, NY

Poo 'Timi

clover honey

Shaken with Belvedere vodka.

Lot 61
New York, NY

Presidente Martini

1 1/2 oz. light rum
1/2 oz. dry vermouth
1 tsp. triple sec
1 to 2 dashes grenadine
lemon twist

Shake liquid ingredients with cracked ice.
Strain into chilled glass. Drop in lemon twist.

Presidente Martini II

1 1/2 oz. light rum
3/4 oz. sweet vermouth
1 1/2 tsp. dry vermouth
dash grenadine
maraschino cherry

Shake liquid ingredients with cracked ice.
Strain into chilled glass. Garnish with
maraschino cherry.

Pressini

chilled martini glass
pour 1 oz. Pernod
fill with 2 oz. fresh chilled espresso

Garnish with 3 white coffee beans.

NY Steakhouse & Pub
Kearny, NJ

Prince's Smile Martini

2 oz. gin
1 oz. apple brandy
1 oz. apricot brandy
1/2 tsp. fresh lemon juice

Shake ingredients with ice. Strain into chilled glass.
*Prince's Grin: Substitute apple juice for the apple brandy and apricot nectar for the apricot brandy.

Princess Mary

1/3 Cork dry gin
1/3 crème de cacao
1/3 fresh cream

Shake.

Princeton Martini

1 1/2 oz. dry gin
1 oz. port
2 dashes orange bitters
twist of lemon peel

Provincetown-Tini

Stolichnaya Ohranj vodka
splash Finlandia cranberry vodka

The Diner on Sycamore
Cincinnati, OH

Psychedelic Martini

6 parts dry gin
1 part French vermouth
1 part Italian vermouth
1/2 part orange juice
1/2 part pineapple juice
dash anisette

Shake.

Puckered Up Apple Kiss

DeKuyper sour apple schnapps
frozen vodka

Serve in chilled martini glass.

Hurricane Restaurant
Passagrille, FL

Pump Martini

Olives, lemon twist, or onions
B&B
1 1/2 oz. vodka
splash dry vermouth

In one mixing glass, marinate the olives, a lemon twist, or onions in B&B. In a second mixing glass combine vodka, vermouth, and several ice cubes. Stir and strain into a chilled martini glass. Garnish with the marinated olives, lemon twist, or onions.

The Pump Room, Chicago, IL
The Complete Book of Mixed Drinks

Punt E Mes Negroni

3/4 oz. dry gin
3/4 oz. sweet vermouth
3/4 oz. Punt E Mes
twist of lemon peel

Pure Martini

....

2 oz. Bombay Sapphire gin
1 tsp. Noilly Prat dry vermouth
2 Spanish cocktail olives for garnish

In a shaker half-filled with ice, combine gin
and vermouth. Shake well, and strain into a
chilled martini glass. Garnish with olives
skewered on a pick.

*The Ritz-Carlton Bar at the Ritz Carlton
San Francisco, CA*

Pure Precipitation Martini

....

2 oz. Rain vodka, chilled

Strain into martini glass. Garnish with slice of
orange.

Rain Vodka

Pure Royalty Martini

....

Royalty vodka
dry vermouth

Garnish with a lemon twist.

*The Martini Bar
Chianti Restaurant, Houston, TX*

Puritan Martini

1 3/4 oz. dry gin
1/2 oz. dry vermouth
1/4 oz. Yellow Chartreuse
dash orange bitters

Purple Haze Martini

2 1/2 oz. vodka
1/2 oz. raspberry liqueur/Chambord
2 oz. sweet and sour
splash 7-Up

Make in pint glass filled with ice. Shake and
serve with strainer and martini glass.

Robert Lehmann, Office Manager
The Broadway Grill, Seattle, WA

Purple Haze Martini II

1/2 oz. vodka
1/2 oz. Chambord
dash triple sec
splash lime juice
splash soda water

Purple Hooter Martini

1/4 shot Chambord
1/4 shot vodka
1/4 shot sour mix
1/4 shot lemon-lime soda

Chill.

Purple Martini

4 oz. Grey Goose vodka
splash Elysium

Mario Arredondo
Biba, Boston, MA

Purple Mask

1 1/2 oz. Smirnoff vodka
1 oz. grape juice
splash white crème de cacao

Chill and strain into chilled martini glass.

Purple People Eater

2 oz. Bacardi Limon
3 oz. cranberry juice
dribble of blue curacao
splash Martini & Rossi extra dry vermouth

Shake with ice. Strain into chilled glasses.

Purple Rain Martini

1 part Rain vodka, chilled
1 part Chambord, chilled

Strain into martini glass. Garnish with twist of
lime.

Rain Vodka

Purpletini

2 oz. Absolut Kurant
1/2 oz. Chambord
1/2 oz. triple sec

Garnish with lemon twist.

Mark Prouty
Ground Round, Framingham, MA

Quatrini Martini

Chocolate martini garnished with chocolate
pennies.

Lot 61
New York, NY

Queen Elizabeth Martini

1 1/2 oz. Bombay gin
dash Martini & Rossi extra dry vermouth
splash Benedictine

Stir in cocktail glass. Strain and serve straight
up or on the rocks. Add lemon twist or olives.

Queen Martini

2 parts dry gin
1 part Italian vermouth
1 part French vermouth
dash orange bitters
dash Angostura bitters

Queenie-Tini

Absolut Kurant vodka
Chambord
champagne

The Diner on Sycamore
Cincinnati, OH

R & R Martini

1 1/2 oz. Gordon's vodka
dash Aquavit

R.A.C.

2 oz. Cork dry gin
1/4 oz. dry vermouth
1 maraschino cherry and twist of orange
dash orange bitters
dash grenadine

Mix.

Racquet Club Martini

1 3/4 oz. dry gin
3/4 oz. dry vermouth
dash orange bitters
orange peel

Radartini

2 parts Smirnoff vodka
1 part tomato juice
olive

The Windsock Bar & Grill
San Diego, CA

Ragazzi Che Martini

2 oz. Belvedere vodka
1/4 oz. Godiva liqueur
1/4 oz. apricot brandy
grapefruit juice

Mad 28
New York, NY

Raidme Martini

1 3/4 oz. dry gin
1/2 oz. Pernod
1/4 oz. Campari

Rainforest Martini

1 part Rain vodka, chilled
1 part Midori melon liqueur
splash 7-Up

Strain into martini glass. Garnish with twist of lime.

Rain Vodka

Rainier Martini

12 sour cherries
1 oz. Belvedere vodka
1 Calvados-marinated bing cherry for garnish

Combine sour cherries with the vodka and let stand 24 hours. Stir well with ice and strain into an ice-cold martini glass. Garnish with the Calvados-marinated bing cherry.

Garden Court at the Four Seasons Olympic Hotel
Seattle, WA

Rain Love Martini

1 oz. Rain vodka
1/2 oz. white crème de cacao
1/4 oz. Chambord

Chill and serve in classic martini glass.

Marcovaldo Dionysas, Bartender
Absinthe Bar & Restaurant, San Francisco, CA

Ranch Style Martini

vodka or gin
Patron tequila

Serve with a pickled olive.

Sheraton Seattle
Seattle, WA

Rasbertini

Stoli Razberi vodka
dash Stoli Ohranj vodka
orange slice garnish

Renaissance Atlanta Hotel
Atlanta, GA

Raschocolate Martini

1 1/2 oz. Smirnoff vodka
1 oz. white crème de cacao
dash raspberry liqueur
2 oz. cranberry juice

Chill and strain into chilled martini glass.

Raspberry Chocolate Martini

1 1/2 oz. Chambord
1 1/2 oz. white crème de cacao

Shake, top with raspberry. Serve straight up or on the rocks.

Joseph Vuckovic
Russo's on the Bay, Howard Beach, NY

Raspberry Martini

1 part Godiva liqueur
1 part Absolut vodka
splash Chambord

Combine with ice and shake well. Serve in a glass whose rim has been dipped in powdered sugar.

Raspberry Martini II

1/2 oz. Monin raspberry syrup
1 1/2 oz. gin or vodka

Pour over ice. Garnish with lemon twist or olive.

Monin Special Cocktail Recipes

Raspberry Martini III

2 oz. Smirnoff vodka
splash raspberry liqueur

Chill, strain, and top with fresh raspberries.

Raspberry Truffle

1 shot Tangueray Sterling vodka
1/2 oz. Baileys Irish Cream
1/2 oz. Kahlúa
1/2 oz. Chambord
mist Martini & Rossi extra dry vermouth

Shake. Serve in iced martini glass. Garnish with cocoa powder on the rim of the glass, a chocolate stick, and raspberry.

Raspberry Twist Martini

1 1/2 oz. Ketel One vodka
1/4 oz. Chambord
Bonny Doon Framboise infusion (local product)
fresh raspberries

Polo Lounge
Windsor Court Hotel, New Orleans, LA

Raspberry Vodka Martini

2 oz. Stoli Razberi vodka
splash Chambord liqueur

Shake with ice and strain into chilled martini
glass. Garnish with lime twist.

Jason Wingerter
Peroni Waterfront Restaurant

Rattler Martini

3/4 oz. dry gin
3/4 oz. French vermouth
3/4 oz. Italian vermouth
1/2 oz. orange juice

Rattlesnake Martini

2 oz. Stoli Cristall vodka
1/4 oz. Chambord
2 splashes cranberry
1 splash pineapple
squeeze lemon and lime

Shake and serve straight up with a twist.

Bobby Carroll
Rattlesnake Bar & Grill, Boston, MA

Razzle Dazzle

1 oz. Stoli Razberi vodka
splash Chambord

Garnish with lemon twist.

Peggy Howell
Cotati Yacht Club & Saloon, Cotati, CA

Real Gordon's Martini

Gordon's vodka
dry vermouth
lemon twist

Red Apple Martini

3/4 oz. dry gin
3/4 oz. sweet vermouth
1/2 oz. apple brandy
1/2 oz. grenadine

Re-Bar Red

2 oz. Campari
juice two lime wedges
juice two lemon wedges
splash 7-up

Red Gin-Gin Martini

dry vermouth
3 oz. gin
1 oz. sloe gin
1 spiral orange twist for garnish

Stir with ice and strain into chilled martini glass. Garnish with spiral orange twist.

The Mandarin
San Francisco, CA

Red-Hot Martini

vodka
cinnamon schnapps
hint Romana sambuca

Serve with Red Hots.

Red Martini

2 oz. Beefeater gin
1/10 oz. dry vermouth
dash Campari

Shake over ice and strain into a chilled martini glass. Garnish with a lemon.

Red Martini II

dash grenadine
1 1/2 oz. gin
1/2 oz. sloe gin

Red Nut

Stoli vodka
splash Frangelico

Hotel San Remo
Las Vegas, CA

Red Passion Martini

1 1/2 oz. Alize
1/2 oz. Campari

Stir well and serve like a martini. Garnish with orange peel.

Red Rim Martini

1 oz. Gordon's vodka
1 1/2 oz. raspberry-white grape juice
blackberry garnish

Rim glass with sweet vermouth. Dip rim in red sugar.

Red Room Martini

4 oz. Stoli Razberi vodka
1 oz. Alize Red Passion
splash sour mix

Shake and serve with twist.

Bob Albright
Le Cirque 2000, New York, NY

Red Royal Martini

Crown Royal whiskey
amaretto

Portland's Best
Portland, OR

Redwood Room Martini

3 oz. Grey Goose vodka
3 olives, one stuffed with Gorgonzola cheese
1 eye drop vermouth

Joe Watts
The Clift Hotel's Redwood Room, San Francisco, CA

Reebok Martini

2 1/2 oz. Skyy vodka
1/2 oz. peach schnapps
1/2 oz. Martini & Rossi extra dry vermouth
lemon twist soaked in Grand Marnier

Reebok Sports Club

Reform Cocktail Martini

1 1/2 oz. dry sherry
3/4 oz. dry vermouth
dash orange bitters
maraschino cherry

Stir liquid ingredients with ice. Strain into
chilled glass. Garnish with maraschino cherry.

Rendezvous Martini

1 1/2 oz. dry gin
1/2 oz. Kirschwasser
1/4 oz. Campari
twist of lemon peel

Richmond Martini

1 3/4 oz. dry gin
3/4 oz. Lillet
twist of lemon peel

Rising Sun Martini

Skyy vodka with a mist of Grand Marnier
orange twist.

Serve up in an oversized chilled stem.
Shaken, not stirred.

Robin's Nest

1 1/2 oz. Smirnoff vodka
1 oz. cranberry juice
splash white crème de cacao

Chill and strain into martini glass.

Robyn's Blue Bomber

2 oz. Beefeater gin
1 drop dry vermouth
1/4 oz. blue curacao

In iced shaker, shake and strain in chilled
martini glass.

Robyn Suchowski
Elizabeth, NJ

Rockefeller

Hennessy VS
Stoli Cristall vodka
champagne
lemon twist

Coat inside of chilled martini glass with
Hennessy, discard excess. Mix Stoli in a mixing tin and stir. Add cold champagne just
before straining into glass. Garnish with
lemon twist.

Matthew Milani
Pittsburgh, PA

Roller Derby Martini

1 3/4 oz. dry gin
1/4 oz. dry vermouth
1/4 oz. sweet vermouth
1/4 oz. Benedictine

Rolls Royce Martini

2 oz. dry gin
1 oz. sweet vermouth
1/2 oz. Benedictine
1/2 oz. dry vermouth

Shake and strain.

Roma Martini

1 1/2 oz. dry gin
1/2 oz. sweet vermouth
1/2 oz. dry vermouth
3 fresh strawberries—mix with drink

Rosa Martini

1 1/2 oz. Bombay gin
dash Martini & Rossi extra dry vermouth
Hiram Walker cherry flavored brandy

Stir in cocktail glass. Strain and serve straight
up or on the rocks. Add lemon twist or olives.

Rosalin Russell Martini

1 1/2 oz. Bombay gin
dash aquavit

Stir in cocktail glass. Strain and serve straight
up or on the rocks. Add lemon twist or olives.

Rose du Boy

1 1/2 oz. dry gin
1/2 oz. dry vermouth
1/4 oz. cherry flavored brandy
1/4 oz. Kirschwasser

Rose Kennedy Martini

1 1/2 oz. vodka
1 oz. peach schnapps
3 oz. lemonade (preferably fresh squeezed)
splash cranberry juice

Fill blender with ice; add all ingredients.
Blend and pour into glass. Garnish with lime
wedge.

Patrick Ford
Smith & Wollensky's, NY, NY

Rose Marie Martini

1 1/4 oz. dry gin
1/2 oz. dry vermouth
1/4 oz. Armagnac
1/4 oz. cherry-flavored brandy
1/4 oz. Campari

Rose Petal

Belvedere vodka
Grand Marnier
Martini & Rossi extra dry vermouth

Garnish with real rose petals.

Iggy's
Chicago, IL

Roselyn Martini

1 1/2 oz. Bombay gin
dash Martini & Rossi extra dry vermouth
Rose's grenadine

Stir in cocktail glass. Strain and serve straight up or on the rocks. Add lemon twist or olives.

Rose's Martini

1 1/2 oz. Absolut vodka
splash Rose's lime juice
splash Chambord

Mix in shaker glass with ice. Strain into martini glass. Serve with a lime.

Donna Eldridge, Bar Manager
Spuds Restaurant & Put, Danvers, MA

Royal Cocktail Martini

1 3/4 oz. dry gin
3/4 oz. Dubonnet
dash orange bitters
dash Angostura bitters

Royal Devil

Stoli Razberi vodka
Chambord
Blackhaus liqueur

Served chilled and straight up.

285

Royal Romance

1 1/2 oz. Cork dry gin
1/4 oz. Grand Marnier
1/2 oz. passion fruit juice
dash sugar syrup

Royal Wedding Martini

Tangueray gin or Stolichnaya vodka
handsomely married to a dash of Chivas
Regal.

Oliver's Mayflower Park Hotel
Seattle, WA

Ruby Slipper Martini

2 oz. Bombay Sapphire
1/4 oz. Grand Marnier
1 or 2 splashes grenadine
dash peppermint schnapps

Garnish with a mint leaf (set it on the edge of
the drink and let it stick out).

Rum Martini

5 parts light rum
1 part French vermouth
twist of lemon peel

Runyons Martini

3 oz. Stoli Ohranj vodka
dash dry vermouth

Stir over ice. Serve straight up in a chilled
martini glass. Garnish with a slice of orange.

Ruski Limonnade

1 oz. Stoli Limonnaya vodka
splash simple syrup

Garnish with lemon twist.

Peggy Howell
Cotati Yacht Club & Saloon, Colati, CA

Russian Brushfire

Stoli Pertsovka vodka
dash Tabasco
bloody mary mix
1 mini jalapeno pepper

Mix Stoli and small portion of bloody mary
mix with ice (enough to make drink red in
color). Shake and strain into chilled martini
glass. Garnish with pepper and dash of
Tabasco.

Matthew Milani
Pittsburgh, PA

Russian Delight Martini

Stoli Vanil vodka with splash of Disaronno amaretto chilled.

Russian Malted Martini

2 oz. Stoli Cristall vodka
1/4 oz. Lagavulin
    (or comparable single malt scotch)

Garnish with a twist.

Russian Martini

3/4 oz. Stoli vodka
3/4 oz. gin
3/4 oz. white crème de cacao

Chill, strain, and serve in a chilled martini glass.

Russian Martini II

Stoliychnaya Ohranj vodka
champagne
orange zest

Martini's
New York, NY

Russian Tiramisu

Stoli Kafya and Vanil vodka

S'more Martini

Finlandia vodka
chocolate liqueur
Martini & Rossi Rosso vermouth

Serve in martini glass rim dipped in cinnamon.

Sake Martini

Belvedere vodka

Shaken with a dash of sake and gin.
Garnished with a cucumber.

Sake Martini II

Stoli Ohranj vodka
splash dry sake
cucumber slice garnish

Saketini Martini

2 oz. dry gin
1/2 oz. sake
twist of lemon peel

Sakitini Martini II

1 1/2 oz. Bombay gin
dash sake

Stir in cocktail glass. Strain and serve straight
up or on the rocks. Add lemon twist or olives.
                    OR
Shake, strain, and serve straight up or on the
rocks with some ice.

Sakitini Martini III

1 1/2 oz. Smirnoff vodka at room temperature
top with 2 1/2 oz. hot sake

Garnish with pickled ginger and a dollop of
Wasabi.

Salome Martini

1 oz. dry gin
3/4 oz. dry vermouth
3/4 oz. Dubonnet

Salt N' Pepper

Absolut Peppar vodka martini with cocktail
onions.

Serve in chilled glass with salted rim.

Cecilia's
Breckenridge, CO

Sam I Am Martini

1 1/4 oz. Absolut Citron vodka
1/4 oz. amaretto
3 oz. cranberry juice

Shake and serve straight up in martini glass
with twist of lemon.

Sambonn Lek, Head Bartender
Renaissance Mayflower Hotel, Washington, DC

San Francisco Cocktail Martini

3/4 oz. sloe gin
3/4 oz. dry vermouth
3/4 oz. sweet vermouth
dash Angostura bitters
dash orange bitters
maraschino cherry

Shake liquid ingredients with ice. Strain into
chilled glass. Drop in maraschino cherry.

San Martin Martini

3/4 oz. dry gin
3/4 oz. dry vermouth
3/4 oz. sweet vermouth
1/4 oz. anisette
dash bitters

Sapphire Martini

Bombay Sapphire gin
Cinzano vermouth

Garnish with an olive.

Sapphire Martini II

Bombay Sapphire
pearl onions

Polo Lounge
Windsor Court Hotel, New Orleans, LA

Saratoga Martini

1 1/2 oz. Smirnoff vodka
2 dashes grenadine
2 dashes Angostura bitters
splash soda water

Garnish with pineapple wedge.

Sargasso Martini

2 oz. Skyy vodka
1/4 oz. Midori
1/4 oz. blue curacao

Garnish with lime twist.

Sassy Jo

Bombay gin
sweet and dry vermouths
splash of orange juice and bitters

Brasserie Jo Martini's
Chicago, IL

Satan's Whiskers

1/2 oz. gin
1/2 oz. dry vermouth
1/4 oz. sweet vermouth
1/2 oz. orange juice
1/4 oz. Grand Marnier
dash orange bitters or orange peel twists

Shake and strain into cocktail glass. Garnish
with orange slice and red maraschino cherry.

Charlie Chop
US Bartenders' Guild, Las Angeles, CA

Sauza Breeze Martini

Sauza tequila
Chambord
sour mix
lime

Gatsby
Boca Raton, FL

Savoy Hotel Special Martini

1 1/2 oz. dry gin
1/2 oz. dry vermouth
dash Pernod
2 dashes grenadine
twist of lemon peel

Savoy Martini

1 3/4 oz. dry gin
1/2 oz. dry vermouth
1/4 oz. Dubonnet
orange peel

Savoy Martini II

Infuse Smirnoff vodka with ripe Bartlett pears
2 oz. infused Smirnoff vodka

Chill, strain, and garnish with a fresh pear
slice.

Scarlettini

Ketel One vodka
touch of Bonny Doon's raspberry wine

Glenn's Restaurant & Cool Bar
Newburyport, MA

Schnozzle Martini

3/4 oz. dry gin
3/4 oz. dry vermouth
1/2 oz. cocktail sherry
1/4 oz. Pernod
1/4 oz. orange curacao

Scotland Yard Martini

Tangueray
splash scotch

No. 18
New York, NY

Sea Spray Martini

Leyden dry gin
Midori melon liqueur
pineapple juice

Red Lobster
Memphis, TN

Sean Lapp Martini

Tangueray Sterling vodka
bleu cheese olives
onion olives

Yvette Wintergarden
Chicago, IL

295

Seduction Martini

1 1/2 oz. Smirnoff vodka
splash brandy
splash Benedictine
1/3 oz. bar lime
splash grenadine

Strain and garnish with orange wheel.

Seed 'N Zest 'Tini

Fennel seed
orange zest freshly ground and shaken with
    Belvedere vodka

Lot 61
New York, NY

Self-Starter Martini

1 1/2 oz. dry gin
3/4 oz. Lillet
1/4 oz. apricot-flavored brandy
2 dashes Pernod

Seventh Heaven Martini

1 1/2 oz. gin
1/2 oz. maraschino cherry juice
1/2 oz. unsweetened grapefruit juice
mint sprig

Shake liquid ingredients with ice. Strain into chilled glass. Drop in orange twist.

Seventh Regiment Martini

1 3/4 oz. dry gin
3/4 oz. sweet vermouth
2 twists of lemon peel

Stir twists with drink.

Sex on the Beach

Frïs vodka
Midori melon liqueur
Chambord
pineapple juice

Gatsby
Boca Raton, FL

Sexual Trance Martini

Absolut Citron vodka
Midori
Chambord
orange juice
pineapple juice
sweet and sour

Garnish with a maraschino cherry.

Sexy Devil

2 parts Finlandia vodka
1 part Finlandia cranberry vodka (infused
    with fresh strawberries)
dash Martini & Rossi extra dry vermouth

Garnish with lemon peel wrapped "Holland"
pepper.

Centro Ristorante
Chicago, IL

Shaken Not Stirred Martini

Tangueray gin
Ketel One vodka
Lillet
lemon twist

Yvette Wintergarden
Chicago, IL

Shampoo for the Beautiful

2 parts Martini & Rossi dry vermouth
1 part vodka
3 parts champagne

Serve in long glass with plenty of ice.

Raymond Taylor
Kent, UK

Sharkbite Martini

Leyden dry gin
Sprite
squeeze of lemon

Red Lobster
Memphis, TN

Sharp Susie Martini

1 part Finlandia Arctic cranberry vodka
1 part Absolut Kurant vodka
1 part Absolut Citron vodka
1 part Cointreau

Shake well and pour into an ice-cold cocktail glass. Garnish with a pearl onion.

Krisu
Email

Sherry Cocktail Martini

2 oz. dry sherry
1/2 oz. dry vermouth
2 dashes orange bitters

Shiso & Lime Leaf Martini

Muddle 3 lime leaves and 2 Shiso leaves with
a large dash of sugar syrup.
Add a large pour of Ketel One vodka.

Shake well. Strain through martini glass.
Garnish with one Shiso and one lime leaf in
the martini glass.

Ben Pundole, General Manager,
Lot 61, New York, NY

Sifi Flip

1 oz. Cork dry gin
1/4 oz. Cointreau
1/4 oz. grenadine
juice of 1/2 lemon
yolk of egg

Shake and strain.

Silk Panties Martini

Smooth blend of Stoli vodka and peach
schnapps.

Silk Spirit

1 oz. Stoli Vanil vodka
1/2 oz. Wild Spirit
1/4 oz. chocolate liqueur

Serve chilled and straight up.

Silken Veil Martini

1 oz. vodka
1 oz. Dubonnet Rouge

Chill, strain, and garnish with a lemon twist.

Silver Bikini Martini

2 oz. Gordon's orange vodka
splash Framboise

Fill shaker with ice, shake, and strain into
martini glass. Garnish with raspberry.

Silver Bullet Martini

1 1/2 oz. Bombay gin
dash Martini & Rossi extra dry vermouth

Shake, strain, and serve straight up or on the
rocks with some ice. Float J&B scotch on top.

Silver Streak Martini

1 1/2 oz. dry gin
1 1/2 oz. Kummel

Pour over finely crushed ice in small wine glass.

Simpson Martini

2 oz. vodka
3/4 oz. vermouth

Mix over ice and shake well. Pour into traditional martini glass. Garnish with sliver of orange peel and black olive speared with dagger plastic toothpick

Karen Pike Davis
Easton, PA

Sky Martini

2 1/2 oz. Skyy vodka
splash blue curacao

Shake over ice and strain into well-chilled glass. Garnish with 2 olives.

The Boulder's Inn
Roxbury, CT

Skyy High Martini

2 oz. Skyy vodka
1/4 oz. Martini & Rossi dry vermouth

Shake with ice and strain into a martini glass
with a jumbo olive.

Heart & Soul
San Francisco, CA

Skyy Blue Buddha

2 oz. Skyy vodka
1/4 oz. sake
1/4 oz. grapefruit juice
1/4 oz. blue curacao
1/2 oz. lemon juice
1/2 oz. lime juice
splash simple syrup

Garnish with fresh orange slice.

301 Sake Bar and Restaurant
San Francisco, CA

Skyy High Martini

Skyy vodka
raspberry liqueur
lemon twist

The Windsock Bar & Grill
San Diego, CA

Skyy White Chocolate Martini

Skyy vodka
white crème de cacao

Serve straight up in an oversized, chilled stem glass. Shaken, not stirred.

Skyy Martini List

Skyy-Fi Martini

2 1/2 oz. Skyy vodka
1/2 oz. Midori
1/2 oz. blue curacao

Chilled and served straight up with lemon twist.

Diane Moscato
7 Central Public House, Manchester, MA

Sloe Vermouth Martini

1 oz. sloe gin
1 oz. dry vermouth
2 tsp. fresh lemon juice

Shake ingredients with ice. Strain into chilled glass.

Smashed Pumpkin

1 oz. Godiva liqueur
1/2 oz. Godet white chocolate liqueur
1/2 oz. Cointreau
1/2 oz. Grey Goose vodka

Garnish with chocolate orange slice.

Jill Ruggles and Erica Holm
Drink, Chicago, IL

Smiler Martini

1 1/4 oz. dry gin
1/2 oz. dry vermouth
1/2 oz. sweet vermouth
1/4 oz. orange juice
dash Angostura bitters

Shake.

Smirnoff Nutcracker Martini

2 oz. Smirnoff vodka
1/2 oz. almond liqueur

Chill, strain, and serve in a martini glass.
Garnish with almonds.

Smokey Martini

Tangueray gin
Scotch
lemon twist

Yvette Wintergarden
Chicago, IL

Smokey Martini II

Coat a martini glass with a good whiskey,
discard excess. Make a normal vodka martini
(shaken not stirred); add to glass.

Mark Wijman
Almere, The Netherlands

Smokey Mountain Martini

1 1/2 oz. Finlandia vodka
1/4 oz. Knob Creek bourbon

Shake and strain into martini glass.

Brett Egan, Director
National Bartenders School, Lakewood, CA

Smooth Operator

2 oz. O.P. Anderson
1/2 oz. Irish cream
1/2 oz. coffee liqueur
1/2 oz. white crème de menthe

Shake with ice. Serve on the rocks or in a
martini glass.

Smooth Martini

Ketel One vodka

Fill shaker with half ice cubes and half shaved
ice. Shake and strain into chilled martini
glass.

Snowball Martini

1 1/2 oz. gin
1/2 oz. Pernod or other anise-flavored liqueur
1/2 oz. cream

Shake ingredients with ice. Strain into chilled
glass.

Snowcone Martini

1 oz. Bacardi spice rum
1 oz. banana liqueur
1/2 oz. blue curacao
mist Martini & Rossi extra dry vermouth

Garnish with a large ball of ice in the middle
of the cocktail.

Michael Jordans
Chicago, IL

Snyder Martini

1 3/4 oz. dry gin
1/2 oz. dry vermouth
1/4 oz. orange curacao
orange peel

So-Co-Martini

2 oz. Southern Comfort
1/4 oz. sweet vermouth
1/4 oz. dry vermouth
maraschino cherry

No. 18
New York, NY

Solar Flare Martini

1 1/2 oz. Tangueray gin
1/4 oz. dry vermouth

Shake and strain. 5 drops of creme de noyaux.
Garnish with maraschino cherry stem.

Doug Bravo
Texas Station Hotel & Casino, Las Vegas, NV

Some Like It Hot Martini

2 oz. Absolut Peppar vodka
red chili pepper

Yvette Wintergarden
Chicago, IL

Some Mother Martini

1 3/4 oz. dry gin
1/2 oz. dry vermouth
1/4 oz. Pernod
cocktail onion

Sonic Gold Martini

1 1/2 oz. Stolichnaya Gold vodka
1 1/2 oz. Campari
splash cranberry juice
splash tonic
soda water to fill glass
orange slice

Pour all ingredients, except soda water, over
ice in a tall glass. Fill rest of the glass with soda
water. Stir and garnish with orange slice.

C3 Restaurant & Lounge
New York, NY

Soprano

2 oz. O.P. Anderson
1/4 oz. dry vermouth
float sambuca on top

Serve on the rocks.

Soprano Royal

2 oz. O.P. Anderson
1/4 oz. Campari

Shake with ice. Serve straight up or on the
rocks.

Sour Apple Martini

2 oz. Grey Goose vodka
1/2 oz. apple pucker schnapps

Garnish with slice of Granny Smith apple.

Michael Waller
Martuni's, San Francisco, CA

Sour Kisses Martini

1 1/2 oz. Bombay gin
dash Martini & Rossi extra dry vermouth
add egg white

Strain and serve straight up or on the rocks.
Add lemon twist or olive.

Sour Patch Martini

2 oz. each Stoli Ohranj, Razberi, Strasberi vodka
splash of pineapple, sour mix, orange juice,
    and grenadine

Gatsby
Boca Raton, FL

South Beach

2 oz. Bacardi rum
1/2 oz. Malibu
1/2 oz. pineapple juice
1/4 oz. blue curacao

Gatsby
Boca Raton, FL

Southern Gin Cocktail Martini

2 1/4 oz. dry gin
1/4 oz. orange curacao
2 dashes orange bitters

Soviet Martini

2 oz. Smirnoff vodka
1/2 oz. Manzanilla sherry
splash dry vermouth

Chill, strain, and garnish with a lemon twist.

Soviet Slush

2 parts Stoli Ohranj vodka
1 part gin
1 part Rumple Minze
1 part Black Haus blackberry schnapps
2 scoops rainbow sherbet

Mix in blender and serve in hurricane glass.
Garnish with piece of kiwi fruit and mint leaf.

Eric Morris
Mulligans, Salisbury, MD

Spanish Martini

1/2 oz. dry sack sherry
1 1/2 oz. gin
twist of lemon

Blend and stir.

Spiced Oyster Martini

fresh Kumamoto oyster covered with jalepeno
    and Tabasco
lemon juice
frozen Belvedere vodka

Lot 61
New York, NY

Spicy Hard Shell Favorite

1 1/2 oz. Stoli Pertsovka vodka
3 dashes Texas Pete hot sauce

Jeff McCarthy
The Hard Shell, Richmond, VA

Sphinx Martini

2 oz. Beefeater gin
1/4 oz. sweet vermouth
3/4 oz. dry vermouth
lemon wedge

Spiaggi

Stolichnaya Vanil vodka
Tuaca Italian liqueur

Maureen & Stephen Horn
Mermaid Martini Bar, Spiaggi, Cape May, NJ

St. Tropez Martini

1 1/2 oz. Smirnoff vodka
splash peach schnapps
splash orange juice
dash grenadine

Chill, strain, and garnish with a fresh peach
wedge.

Stake Martini

vodka, shaken
dash sake
dash gin

Garnished with cucumber.

Lot 61
New York, NY

Stang Bill Martini

1 1/2 oz. Tangueray gin poured into glass
shaker with ice. Wash martini glass with The
Famous Grouse. Roll shaker with gin back
and forth mixing gin into ice. Top shaker with
ice and strain gin into glass using ice as
strainer. Garnish with olives.

Bill Stang, Bartender
The Blackduck Freehouse, Saskatchewan, BC

Star Cocktail Martini

1 1/2 oz. apple brandy
1 1/2 oz. sweet vermouth
2 dashes Angostura bitters
lemon twist

Stir liquid ingredients with ice. Strain into
chilled glass. Drop in lemon twist.

Starry Night

2 oz. Vincent vodka
1/2 oz. blue curacao
splash sweet and sour

Combine ingredients and pour into a martini glass. Garnish with lemon twist.

Andy Porter
Van Gogh's Restaurant & Bar, Atlanta, GA

Star Tini

Rinse glass with Martini & Rossi extra dry
    vermouth
2 1/2 oz. Stoli Cristall vodka
1/2 oz. Campari

Orange twist to garnish.

Harry Denton's Starlight Room
San Francisco, CA

Starburst Martini

2 oz. Grey Goose vodka
1 oz. strawberry liqueur
1/2 oz. pineapple juice
1/2 oz. sour mix
pinch of sugar

Mix all ingredients and shake vigorously.
Serve with a strawberry.

"Smiley"
Bash Nightclub, Miami, FL

Starlight Martini

1 3/4 oz. Beefeater gin
3/4 oz. orange curacao
dash Angostura bitters

Shake.

Startini

2 oz. Belvedere vodka
few drops of Edmond Briottet
mandarin liqueur

Rinse glass with dry vermouth. Stirred, not
shaken. Garnish with orange zest.

Jeramiah Tower's Stars Restaurant
San Francisco, CA

Stefano Martini

1 1/2 oz. Smirnoff vodka
float lemonade
dash grenadine

Chill and strain into a martini glass.

Sterling Gold Martini

Tangueray Sterling vodka
touch Tuaca
zest of orange

Oliver's Mayflower Park Hotel
Seattle, WA

Stick 'Em Up

Equal parts:
    Cactus Juice liqueur
    vodka

Still Life Martini

2 oz. Smirnoff vodka
1/4 oz. coffee liqueur
1/4 oz. Baileys Irish Cream

Combine. Strain and garnish with an orange
wheel and maraschino cherry.

Stoli Bellini Martini

champagne
Stoli Persik vodka
splash peach schnapps

Stoli Bikini Martini

3 oz. of Stoli Ohranj vodka
generous splash Framboise

Fill shaker with ice and shake or stir vigorously. Strain liquid into martini glasses.
Garnish with raspberry.

Stoli Grand Martini

2 oz. dry vermouth in tumbler with crushed ice
drain off vermouth
1 1/2 oz. Stoli Ohranj vodka
1/4 oz. Grand Marnier

Swirl in tumbler for 2–3 minutes until silky.

Jay Tarantino
Taverne on the Lake, Lawrenceburg, IN

Stoli Hummer

1 oz. Stoli Vanil vodka
1 oz. amaretto
1 oz. Bacardi rum
1/2 oz. grenadine
2 oz. orange juice

Fill shaker with ingredients and shake. Strain
into tall glass filled with ice.

Andrew Thompson
Rock & Kath's Sawmill

Stoli Kafya Martini

Stoli Kafya vodka
Stoli Vanil vodka

Serve in a chilled martini glass or over rocks.

Stoli Oh What a Night Martini

1 1/2 oz. Stoli Ohranj vodka
splash Caffe Sport espresso liqueur

Shake ingredients and strain into a cocktail
glass. Garnish with orange slice.

Stoli Power Martini

1 1/2 oz. Stoli Ohranj vodka
1/2 oz. lemon juice
3 oz. orange juice
1 oz. raspberry syrup

Pour ingredients into a mixing glass, add ice, and shake well. Strain into a chilled glass and garnish with an orange peel.

Stolichnaya Paradise Martini

2 parts Stoli Ohranj vodka
1 part orange juice

Shake ingredients with ice. Pour into a martini glass. Garnish with an orange slice.

Straight Law Martini

1 3/4 oz. dry sherry
3/4 oz. dry gin
twist of lemon peel

Strawberry Blintz Martini

2 oz. Stoli Strasberi vodka
splash cranberry

Serve shaken with a sugar-rimmed martini glass. Garnish with white chocolate dipped strawberry.

Strawberry Blonde Martini

2 oz. Beefeater gin
1 oz. Chambraise strawberry aperitif
twist of lemon peel

Strawberry Chocolate Martini

1 1/2 oz. strawberry liqueur
1 1/2 oz. white crème de cacao

Shake, top with a strawberry. Serve straight up or on the rocks.

Joseph Vuckovic
Russo's on the Bay, Howard Beach, NY

Strawberry Martini

1 1/2 oz. dry gin
1/2 oz. Chambraise
fresh strawberry garnish

Blend and stir.

Super Model

2 oz. Bacardi Limon
1/2 oz. melon liqueur
1/2 oz. blue curacao
splash Martini & Rossi extra dry vermouth

Shake ingredients with ice. Strain into chilled glasses.

String of Pearls

2 1/2 oz. Leyden gin
4 cocktail onions

Bill Chiusano
Bloomfield, NJ

Submarine Martini

1 1/2 oz. dry gin
1/2 oz. Dubonnet
1/2 oz. dry vermouth
dash Boker's bitters

Sugar Magnolia Dark Martini

1 1/4 oz. vodka
3/4 oz. dark crème de cacao

Garnish with a Hershey's Kiss.

Sullivan's Martini

3 oz. Ketel One vodka
1/2 oz. Martini & Rossi extra dry vermouth
Lechee nuts
Goachee nuts

Reebok Sports Club

Summer Martini

3 oz. Gordon's vodka
splash extra dry vermouth
splash cucumber juice
cucumber slice garnish

Summertime Martini

1 1/4 oz. Stoli Ohranj vodka
1 1/4 oz. Gordon's grapefruit gin
1/2 oz. Chambord

Shake and strain straight up or on the rocks.
Garnish with a flag.

Charlie's on the Lake
Omaha, NE

Sunburst Martini

orange vodka
dry vermouth
orange slice

Yvette Wintergarden
Chicago, IL

Sundowner Martini

2 oz. Stoli Razberi vodka
2 1/2 oz. orange juice
1/4 oz. cranberry juice
1 or 2 splashes grenadine

Shake the vodka and orange juice. Strain into glass and add the cranberry juice and grenadine.

Sunflower

2 oz. Vincent vodka
1/2 oz. Grand Marnier
splash blood orange juice

Combine all ingredients and shake with ice. Garnish with blood orange wedge/edible flowers.

Andy Porter
Van Gogh's Restaurant & Bar, Atlanta, GA

Sunrise Martini

2 oz. Smirnoff vodka
1 oz. Cuervo 1800 tequila
splash Grand Marnier
splash grenadine

Garnish with orange slice.

Sunset

Stoli Ohranj vodka
dash bitters

Garnish with an orange slice.

Super Juice Martini

Stoli Ohranj vodka
dash cranberry juice
dash orange juice

Tunnel Bar Raphael
Providence, RI

Supper Martini

2 oz. Boodles gin
dash Drambuie
dash sweet vermouth
1 maraschino cherry for garnish

Shake with ice and strain into a chilled martini
glass. Garnish with maraschino cherry.

Mumbo Jumbo
Atlanta, GA

Supreme Chocolate Martini

2 oz. vodka
1 1/2 oz. Marie Brizard white crème de cacao
unsweetened cocoa powder
1 Hershey's Hug candy

Coat rim with cocoa powder and place the
kiss pointed top up in the bottom of the glass.
Stir in glass of ice until well chilled and strain.

Marie Brizard
Florida

Surfer Martini

1 1/2 oz. Smirnoff vodka
1/2 oz. Malibu coconut rum
splash banana liqueur

Chill, strain, and garnish with a pineapple
wedge.

Sushi Martini

Tangueray gin
Martini & Rossi extra dry vermouth

Serve straight up with a Tobiko stuffed olive
and pickled ginger.

Bruno's Club Deluxe
Chicago, IL

Sweet Arlene

1/4 oz. apple cider
1/4 oz. Martini & Rossi sweet vermouth
1/4 oz. Limoncello
1/4 oz. gin
dash bitters

Garnish with apple slice.

Steve Visakay
Vintage Cocktail Shakers

Sweet Dutchman

2 parts sweet vermouth
1 part Leyden gin
orange peel

Bill Chiusano
Bloomfield, NJ

Sweet Martini

1 1/2 oz. Absolut Citron vodka
1/4 oz. extra dry vermouth
splash Chambord

Combine in a shaker with ice. Shake well and
strain into martini glass. Garnish with twist of
lemon.

Jane Lomshek, Bartender
Holidome, Lawrence, KS

Swiss Kiss Martini

2 oz. Grey Goose vodka
1/2 oz. Frangelico
1/2 oz. butterscotch schnapps
1 oz. crème de cacao
lace with Godet white chocolate liqueur
sprinkle with Godiva chocolate

Iraklis Papachristos of Mercury Bar
Boston, MA

Tango Cocktail Martini

1 oz. gin
1/2 oz. Martini and Rossi vermouth
1/2 oz. Martini and Rossi sweet vermouth
1/2 oz. fresh orange juice
1/2 tsp. triple sec

Shake ingredients with ice. Strain into chilled glass.

Take Off Martini

Tangueray gin
splash Cointreau
orange peel

The Windsock Bar & Grill
San Diego, CA

Tall, Dark, & Handsome

Equal parts:
    crème de cacao
    Buttershots schnapps
    Trilla Vanilla liqueur
    vodka

Glass lightly drizzled with chocolate syrup.

Mindy Moller
Shake-Up Your Martini

Tangerine Delight

Stoli Ohranj vodka
dash dark crème de cacao

Chill and serve up with orange twist.

Shirley Morgan, Bartender
Pier St. Pub, Jupiter, FL

Tangueray Extra Dry Martini

Tangueray gin
dry vermouth

Serve straight up in chilled martini glass.
Garnish with olive.

Hurricane Restaurant
Passagrille, FL

Tangueray "Perfect Ten" Martini

2 oz. Tangueray No. Ten
1 oz. Grand Marnier
1/2 oz. sour mix

Tangueray No. Ten Martini

2 1/4 oz. Tangueray No. Ten
1 3/4 oz. lime juice
squeeze in one lime wedge

Tanqy Breezy Martini

3 oz. Tangueray gin
dash dry vermouth
1 oz. pineapple juice
1 oz. grapefruit juice
lemon twist or olive

Hyman Goldfeld
Philadelphia, PA

Tantra Kiss

3 oz. Grey Goose vodka
1 oz. peach schnapps
splash cranberry juice
splash pineapple juice

Shake with ice and serve straight up with an
edible pansy.

Bruce Craig
Tantra, Inc., Miami, FL

Tapika's Martini

2 1/2 oz. Chinaco Blanco tequila
1/2 oz. Cointreau
1/2 oz. Martini & Rossi extra dry vermouth
lime wedge

Reebok Sports Club

Tartini

1 1/2 oz. Stoli Razberi vodka
dash Chambord
dash Rose's lime juice
splash cranberry juice

Garnish with lime wedge.

Tequila Martini

tequila
Cointreau
Grand Marnier

Tatou's Tatouni

3 oz. Ketel One vodka
Martini & Rossi extra dry vermouth
splash cucumber juice
cucumbers to garnish

Reebok Sports Club

Teeny Weeny Chocolate Martini

Ketel One vodka
white crème de cacao
chocolate truffle garnish

Temple-Tini

Absolut Kurant vodka
sprinkle of Chambord
maraschino cherry

Tequila Gimlet Martini

2 oz. tequila
1 oz. lime juice

Chill, strain, and garnish with a lime wedge.

Tequina Martini

2 oz. tequila
1/2 oz. dry vermouth

Stir tequila and vermouth with ice in a mixing
glass until chilled. Strain into a chilled cocktail
glass. Garnish with lemon twist.

Thai Martini

2 oz. infused Smirnoff vodka

Infuse Smirnoff vodka with lemongrass. Chill, strain, and garnish with a fresh sprig of coriander.

That's Italian Martini

Ketel One vodka
Campari
orange and lemon slice

Yvette Wintergarden
Chicago, IL

The "61" Cosmo

Stoli Razberi vodka
cranberry juice
lime juice
triple sec

Shake. Garnish with raspberries and a twist.

Lot 61
New York, NY

The All-American Martini

1 1/2 oz. Glacier vodka
dash vermouth

Garnish with two olives skewered by an
American flag toothpick.

The "Perfect" Martini

Bombay Sapphire gin
eye-dropper of dry vermouth

Garnish with jumbo shrimp and cocktail
sauce.

Shulas No Name Lounge

The "Q" Martini

2 oz. Smirnoff vodka
splash blue curacao
dash lime juice

Chill, strain, and garnish with a lemon twist.

The 11 Onion Gibson

1/2 oz. Bombay Sapphire gin
2 drops dry vermouth

Garnish with 11 cocktail onions.

Charles McMahan
New Matamoras, OH

The Godfather

Belvedere vodka
Grand Marnier
amaretto
Martini & Rossi extra dry vermouth

Garnish with a maraschino cherry and an
orange twist.

Harry's Velvet Room
Chicago, IL

The Griese Martini

Skyy vodka
Godiva liqueur

Garnish with a Hershey's Kiss.

Shulas No Name Lounge

The Holiday Martini

1 1/2 oz. Finlandia cranberry vodka
1 1/2 oz. Absolut Kurant
1/2 oz. Martini & Rossi sweet vermouth

Garnish with cherry.

Handshakes Bar & Grill
Hopewell Junction, NY

The Horton

Grey Goose vodka
splash orange flower water

The Mark Hauser

Ketel One vodka
splash Chambord

*The Diner on Sycamore
Cincinnati, OH*

Thigh Opener

2 oz. O.P. Anderson
1/4 oz. lime juice
1/4 oz. triple sec

Shake. Serve on the rocks.

Third Degree Martini

2 oz. infused Smirnoff vodka

Infuse Smirnoff vodka with jalapeno pepper
seeds intact. Thoroughly chill vodka in the
freezer. Chill, strain, and garnish with pickled
yellow pepper.

Thrust Martini

Hennessy VS Cognac
dash lemon juice
lemon peel

The Windsock Bar & Grill
San Diego, CA

Three Continents Martini

1 1/4 oz. Skyy vodka
1/4 oz. Grand Marnier
2 drops blue curacao

Shake with ice and strain into chilled martini glass. Garnish with orange twist.

Cliff Inn
El Paso, TX

Thrilla Vanilla Martini

Stoli Vanil vodka straight up

Thunderer Martini

Stolichnaya shaken with blue curacao and cassis.

Lot 61
New York, NY

Tiger-Tini

Stolichnaya Ohranj vodka
Grand Marnier
splash orange juice

The Diner on Sycamore
Cincinnati, OH

Tijuanatini

Ketel One vodka
Kahlúa
coffee beans

Cecilia's
Breckenridge, CO

Tio Pepe Martini

7 parts dry gin
2 parts Tio Pepe sherry
twist of lemon peel

Toasted Almond Martini

2 1/2 oz. Stoli Vanil vodka
1/2 oz. Stoli Kafya vodka
splash amaretto

Garnish with almond or hazelnut.

Tonight or Never Martini

1 oz. dry gin
1 oz. dry vermouth
1/2 oz. cognac

Topaz Martini

1 3/4 oz. Bacardi Limon
1/4 oz. Martini & Rossi extra dry vermouth
splash blue curacao

Combine in a cocktail glass.

Topaz Martini II

5 parts Gordon's vodka
1 part dark crème de cacao
1 part Frangelico

Float 3 whole roasted coffee beans in glass.

Tres Martini

1 1/2 oz. Tres Generaciones
splash Cointreau

Rinse a chilled martini glass with a splash of
Cointreau and discard. Place Tres
Generaciones in a shaker. Fill with ice, shake,
and strain into the prepared glass. Garnish
with orange zest.

Trilby Martini

1 1/4 oz. dry gin
1 oz. sweet vermouth
2 dashes orange bitters

Stir. Float 1/4 oz. creme de yvette on the surface or Chambord.

Trinity Martini

1 oz. dry gin
1 oz. red vermouth
1 oz. dry vermouth

Shake and strain.

Trinity Martini aka
Trio Plaza Martini

1 oz. Bombay gin
1 oz. half Rosso vermouth and half extra dry
    vermouth

Stir in cocktail glass. Strain and serve straight up or on the rocks. Add lemon twist or olives.

Triple G Martini

2 oz. Grey Goose vodka
dash Hershey's syrup in glass
1 oz. Godet or white chocolate liqueur

Shake gently. Garnish with Hershey's syrup.

Erica Frene
The Rack, Boston, MA

Tropical Martini

1 1/2 oz. Smirnoff vodka
splash Malibu rum
splash pineapple juice

Chill, strain, and garnish with pineapple.

Tropical Martini II

2 oz. Malibu or Parrot Bay coconut rum
1/2 oz. pineapple juice
splash Rose's lime juice
dash salt

Shake, add ice, shake again, and strain into
chilled martini glass. Garnish with whatever
fruit is available.

Amanda
Email

Tropical Martini III

Stoli Ohranj and Vanil vodkas
pineapple juice

Renaissance Atlanta Hotel
Atlanta, GA

Tropical Spellbinder

Absolut Citron vodka
blue curacao
Midori

Tropitini Martini

Finlandia vodka
Bacardi Limon
blue curacao
pineapple juice
whisper of Martini & Rossi extra dry vermouth

Shake, strain, and garnish with pineapple.

Martini Ranch
Chicago, IL

Truffle

Absolut Kurant vodka
crème de cacao

Portland's Best
Portland, OR

Tulip Cocktail

3/4 oz. apple brandy
3/4 oz. sweet vermouth
2 tsp. apricot brandy
1 1/2 tsp. fresh lemon juice

Shake ingredients with cracked ice. Strain into chilled glass.

Turantini

1 1/2 oz. Turantula tequila
1/4 oz. Cointreau
splash Rose's lime

Garnish with lime twist.

Tim Parsons
Pegasus, San Antonio, TX

Tuxedo Martini

1 1/4 oz. dry gin
1 1/4 oz. dry vermouth
1/4 oz. maraschino cherry juice
1/4 tsp. Pernod
2 dashes orange bitters
twist of lemon peel

Twisted Breeze Martini

1 1/2 oz. Smirnoff Citrus Twist vodka
dash grapefruit juice
dash cranberry juice

Chill, strain, and serve with fresh cranberries.

Twisted Citrus Martini

2 oz. frozen Smirnoff Citrus Twist vodka

Chill, strain, and garnish with large wedges of lemon and lime squeezed into the vodka.

Twisted Hound Martini

1 1/2 oz. Smirnoff vodka
splash freshly-squeezed pink grapefruit juice

Chill and strain into well-chilled martini glass.

Twisted Plaza Martini

1 1/2 oz. Smirnoff Citrus Twist vodka
dash melon liqueur
splash pineapple juice and orange juice

Chill, strain, and garnish with a fresh pineapple wedge.

Twisted-Tini

Smirnoff Citrus Twist vodka
dry vermouth

Shaken, not stirred.

Martini's
New York, NY

Twisting Kurant

2 oz. Absolut Kurant vodka
big splash sweet vermouth

Strain into chilled martini glass. Serve with
sugar coated lemon twist.

Olive Garden
Lincoln, NE

Two Lips Martini

Leyden gin
splash Chambord

Bill Chiusano
Bloomfield, NJ

Tyne's Martini

3 shots of vodka
twist of lemon
shake gently with ice
dash Captain Morgan spiced rum

Tyne Caouette
Portage, MI

USA Martini

Teton Glacier vodka—made in the USA
splash vermouth

Ultimate Chill

2 1/2 oz. Bombay Sapphire gin or Stolichnaya
    God vodka
1/4 oz. Cinzano dry vermouth

Garnish with 2 large vermouth-marinated
Italian olives.

Marcus Nates & Steve Burney
Oliver's in the Mayflower Park Hotel, Seattle, WA

Ultimate Martini

1 oz. Stoli vodka
1/2 oz. Campari
1/4 oz. sweet vermouth

347

Ultimate Martini II

Boodles British dry gin
whisper of dry vermouth
queen olives stuffed with Stilton cheese

Polo Lounge
Windsor Court Hotel, New Orleans, LA

Under the Volcano Martini

The Encantado Martini—100 percent Mescal
Martini & Rossi vermouth

Garnish with a jalapeno stuffed olive.

Union League Martini

1 3/4 oz. Old Tom gin
3/4 oz. port wine
dash orange bitters

Up Up & Away

Beefeater gin
splash grapefruit juice
lemon twist

The Windsock Bar & Grill
San Diego, CA

Uptown Alize

2 oz. Hennessy
2 oz. Alize Red Passion

Serve over ice.

Sidney Masters
The Shark Bar, New York, NY

Usabay Martini

1 3/4 oz. vodka
1/2 oz. Captain Morgan Parrot Bay coconut rum

Garnish with coconut twist.

Chris Hammond
The Thirsty Turtle, Bernardsville, NJ

USA, Prince of Martini

3/4 oz. vodka
1/2 oz. Wild Spirit
dash vermouth

Garnish with orange wheel.

Steve Prince
The Thirsty Turtle, Bernardsville, NJ

Valerie

Tangueray gin
splash olive juice
Top with 2 olives

Wendy Michaels
Branding Iron, Yamhill, OR

Vampire Martini

2 oz. Stolichnaya vodka
1/2 oz. Chambord
touch of cranberry

No. 18
New York, NY

Van Martini

1 3/4 oz. dry gin
1/2 oz. dry vermouth
1/4 oz. Grand Marnier

Vanilla Beani

1 oz. Stoli Vanil vodka
splash Tuaca

Garnish with vanilla bean.

Peggy Howell
Cotati Yacht Club & Saloon, Cotati, CA

Vanilla Martini

Freshly muddled vanilla beans shaken with Belvedere vodka and sugar.

Lot 61
New York, NY

Vanilla Rain

1 part Rain vodka, chilled
1 part Dr. Vanillacuddy, chilled

Strain into martini glass.

Veggie Martini

2 1/2 oz. Tangueray gin

Garnish with green and black olives, onions, and baby carrots.

Cecilia's
Breckenridge, CO

Velocity Martini

1 1/2 oz. Bombay gin
dash Martini & Rossi extra dry vermouth
add orange slice

Shake, strain, and serve straight up or on the rocks with some ice.

Velour Martini

1 1/2 oz. Smirnoff vodka
splash blue curacao
splash cranberry juice

Chill, strain, and garnish with cranberries.

Velvet Bunny Martini

1 1/2 oz. Smirnoff vodka
dash banana liqueur
Romana Black sambuca

Combine. Strain and garnish with banana slice.

Velvet Citrus Martini

2 1/2 oz. Gordon's citrus vodka
lemon twist

Velvetini

3 oz. Grey Goose vodka
1/2 oz. Poires D'Anjou
dash Disaronno amaretto
dash Godiva dark chocolate liqueur

Shake hard with ice for 1 1/2 minutes. Strain into chilled martini glass. Garnish with one strawberry.

Brady and Dina Martin
Hudson Club, Chicago, IL

Vendome Martini

1 oz. Beefeater gin
1 oz. Dubonnet
1/2 oz. dry vermouth
twist of lemon peel

Vermouth Cassis Martini

2 parts Martini & Rossi dry vermouth
1 part creme de cassis

Pour over ice and stir well.

Vermouth Cocktail

1 oz. dry vermouth
1 oz. sweet vermouth
2 dashes orange bitters
maraschino cherry

Stir liquid ingredients with ice. Strain into
chilled glass. Garnish with maraschino cherry.

Vermouth Rinse Martini

Coat the inside of a glass with dry vermouth.
Shake off the excess. Fill the glass with
chilled Beefeater gin. Add a twist of lemon
peel or green olive.

Vermouth Triple Sec Martini

1 oz. Martini and Rossi dry vermouth
1 oz. dry gin
1/2 oz. triple sec
2 dashes orange bitters
twist of lemon peel

Very Berry Martini

2 oz. gin
1/2 oz. cranberry juice cocktail

Combine in ice-filled shaker. Shake and strain into well-chilled martini glass. Garnish with fresh berry of your choice.

Brigid Heckman
Rexville, NY

Very Dry Martini

5 parts Beefeater gin
1 part French vermouth
twist of lemon peel

Vespers

2 parts Ketel One vodka
1 part Tangueray gin
splash Lillet

Lloyd Heslip
Email

Victor Martini

1 1/2 oz. dry vermouth
1/2 oz. dry gin
1/2 oz. brandy

Viking

2 1/2 oz. Absolut Kurant
1/2 oz. Chambord

Garnish with a twist.

Viking Serum Martini

3 parts classic Finlandia
3 parts seltzer
splash blue curacao
splash cranberry juice

Vilvitini

3 oz. Grey Goose
1/2 oz. Poires D'Anjou
dash Disaronno amaretto
dash Godiva Dark Chocolate liqueur

Shake hard with ice for 1 1/2 minutes. Strain into
chilled martini glass. Garnish with one gooseberry.

Brady and Dina Martin
Hudson Club, Chicago, IL

Violetta

2 1/2 oz. Absolut vodka
1/2 oz. blue curacao
splash cranberry juice

Garnish with a twist.

Vip Martini

Fill a stemmed cocktail glass with chilled dry gin. Waft a fine spray of dry vermouth gently on the surface from an atomizer. Add a twist of lemon peel or a green olive.

Visamini

1 oz. Absolut Kurant
1 oz. Bacardi Limon
1/4 oz. Midori
dash Rose's lime juice

Steve Visakay
Vintage Cocktail Shakers

Vodka Gibson Martini

premium vodka
dash vermouth

Shaken or stirred. Garnish with an onion, or two or three.

Vodka Martini

2 oz. vodka
1/2 oz. dry vermouth
twist of lemon peel or green olive

Voodoo Martini

Chill 2 oz. Smirnoff vodka in shaker.
Thinly slice clove of garlic and place at bottom of the martini glass. Strain vodka into glass. Garnish with lemon wedge.

Vuk's Martini

1 1/2 oz. Baileys Irish Cream
1 1/2 oz. white crème de cacao

Shake, and serve straight up or on the rocks. The best way to have this martini is with ice cream. Put all ingredients in a blender and whip it up.

Joseph Vuckovic
Russo's on the Bay, Howard Beach, NY

Wai Lin Martini

2 oz. Smirnoff vodka
1/4 oz. cranberry juice
1/4 oz. melon liqueur

Strain and garnish with lemon.

Waiting for Godet Martini

2 oz. Smirnoff vodka
dash Godet White Belgium chocolate liqueur
dash bourbon

Chill, strain, and garnish with a fresh strawberry.

Wallet Chain

2 oz. Stoli Pertsovka or Absolut Peppar vodka
dash Worcestershire sauce
splash jalepeno-stuffed olive juice

Garnish with jalepeno olives and pearl onions.

Jim Stacy
The Manhattan Café, Athens, GA

Wallick Martini

1 1/2 oz. Bombay gin
dash Martini & Rossi extra dry vermouth
dash Hiram Walker orange curacao

Stir in cocktail glass. Strain and serve straight
up or on the rocks. Add lemon twist or olives.

Walter Martini

5 parts dry gin
1/2 part dry vermouth
1/2 part dry sherry
2 drops lemon juice

Warden Martini

1 1/2 oz. Bombay gin
dash Martini & Rossi extra dry vermouth
dash Pernod

Stir in cocktail glass. Strain and serve straight
up or on the rocks. Add lemon twist or olives.

Watermelon Martini

2 oz. Absolut Citron
splash Rose's lime juice
4 oz. watermelon juice

Pour over ice and shake vigorously. Strain into
chilled 4 oz. martini glasses.

Watermelon Martini II

5 oz. Grey Goose vodka
1/2 oz. cranberry juice
1/2 oz. sour mix

Wayne's Martini

3 oz. Beefeater gin
1/8 oz. Glen Ord single malt scotch

Stir gently over cracked ice. Strain into chilled 5 oz. martini glass. Garnish with 2 green olives stuffed with anchovy.

Wayne Beckwith
Fairport Village Inn, Fairport, NY

Well, What the People Think Are Martinis!

1 oz. Absolut vodka
1 oz. Bombay gin
5/8 oz. fresh-squeezed lemon juice
1 1/4 oz. Grand Marnier
1 oz. cranberry

Chill in shaker and serve straight up in prechilled martini glass. Garnish with 1/4 inch lemon wheel caramelized with sugar.

Daryle Norberg, Bartender
Byron's Sports Bar, San Leandro, CA

Wembley Martini

1 1/2 oz. dry gin
3/4 oz. dry vermouth
1/4 oz. apple brandy
dash apricot-flavored brandy

West Peachtree Martini

Stolichnaya Persik vodka
dash cranberry juice

Renaissance Atlanta Hotel
Atlanta, GA

White Chocolate Martini

1 1/2 oz. Skyy vodka
1/2 oz. Godiva chocolate liqueur

Chill glass, rim with chocolate shell. Shake
ingredients and pour into chilled, rimmed
glass. Garnish with a Hershey's Hug candy.

Pamela Conaway
Hurricane Restaurant, Passagrille, FL

White Lady

3/4 oz. Cointreau
1 1/2 oz. gin
1/3 oz. lemon juice

Shake with ice. Strain into a martini glass.

Remy Amerique, Inc.
New York, NY

White Russian Martini

2 oz. Smirnoff vodka
1 oz. Kahlúa
1 oz. half and half

Combine. Strain into chilled martini glass.

White Way Cocktail Martini

1 1/2 Beefeater gin
3/4 oz. white crème de menthe

Shake ingredients with cracked ice. Strain
into chilled glass.

Why Not Martini

1 oz. Beefeater gin
1 oz. apricot brandy
1 tsp. lemon juice

Chill, strain, and serve with a lemon twist.

Wild Horse

1 1/2 oz. Stoli Razberi vodka
1/2 oz. amaretto

Serve chilled in martini glass. Garnish with
fresh raspberry.

Ifis Vourlatos
Email

Wild Rose Martini

1 1/2 oz. dry gin
1/2 oz. dry vermouth
1/2 oz. sweet vermouth
dash orange bitters
dash Angostura bitters

Will Rogers Martini

1 1/2 oz. gin
1/2 oz. dry vermouth
1/2 oz. orange juice
1 1/2 tsp. triple sec

Shake ingredients with ice. Strain into chilled glass.

Wilson Special Martini

2 oz. dry gin
1/4 oz. dry vermouth
2 orange slices

Shake.

Windex Martini

1 oz. Ketel One vodka
1/2 oz. Cointreau
1 oz. sour mix
1 oz. 7-Up

Rim glass with lemon and sugar. Shake well and add maraschino cherry.

Lisa McArthur, Cheerleaders
Philadelphia, PA

Windex Martini II

2 1/2 oz. vodka
1/2 oz. blue curacao
2 oz. lemonade

Shake and serve with strainer and martini glass.

Windsock Martini

Absolut Kurant vodka
splash cranberry juice
lemon juice
lemon peel

The Windsock Bar & Grill
San Diego, CA

Xanthia Martini

1 1/2 oz. dry gin
1 oz. dry vermouth
1 oz. Cointreau

Mix and serve on the rocks.

Yachting Club Martini

1 3/4 oz. Holland's gin
3/4 oz. dry vermouth
2 dashes Peychaud's bitters
dash Pernod

Sweeten with sugar to taste.

Yachting Martini

1 1/2 oz. Smirnoff vodka
splash peach schnapps
splash melon liqueur

Chill, strain, and garnish with a fresh peach wedge.

Yale Cocktail Martini

1 1/2 oz. Beefeater gin
1/2 oz. dry vermouth
1 tsp. blue curacao or cherry brandy
dash bitters

Stir.

Yale Martini

1 2/3 oz. Plymouth gin
1/2 oz. dry vermouth
2 dashes orange bitters
1/4 oz. maraschino cherry juice

Sweeten with sugar to taste.

Yang Martini

2 1/2 oz. gin
1/2 oz. sake

Stir with ice and strain into a chilled martini glass.

Inagiku
New York, NY

Yellow Daisy

1 1/2 oz. Beefeater gin
1/2 oz. dry vermouth
1/4 oz. Grand Marnier
1/4 oz. Pernod
maraschino cherry

Yellow Fingers Martini

1 1/2 oz. gin
3/4 oz. blackberry brandy
1/2 oz. crème de banana
1/2 oz. cream

Shake ingredients with ice. Strain into chilled glass.

Yellow Rattler

2 oz. Bombay Sapphire gin
1 oz. extra dry vermouth
dash orange bitters
2 cocktail onions

Ying Martini

2 1/2 oz. sake
1/2 oz. gin

Stir with ice and strain into a chilled martini glass.

Inagiku
New York, NY

Yolanda Martini

3/4 oz. dry gin
3/4 oz. brandy
1/2 oz. sweet vermouth
1/4 oz. grenadine
1/4 oz. Pernod

York Martini

7 parts dry gin
1 part French vermouth
drop scotch
twist of lemon peel

Yukon Martini

2 oz. Smirnoff vodka
dash Yukon Jack to coat the martini glass

Chill and strain vodka into the coated martini glass. Garnish with a lemon wedge.

Yvette Martini

Ketel One vodka
Grand Marnier

Garnish with an orange twist.

Yvette Wintergarden
Chicago, IL

Zanzibar Martini

2 1/2 oz. dry vermouth
1 oz. gin
1/2 oz. lemon juice
1 tsp. sugar syrup
3 dashes bitters

Chill, strain, and garnish with a lemon twist.

Zara Martini

1 3/4 oz. Old Tom gin
3/4 oz. Dubonnet
dash orange bitters

Zinamartini

1 1/2 oz. Stoli Zinamon vodka
1/4 oz. dry vermouth

Pour vermouth into glass. Discard vermouth
and add Stoli. Garnish with cinnamon stick.
Serve in martini glass.

Joe Chironno
Celebrity Pub, Wheatley Heights, NY

Zinamon Toast Martini

2 oz. Stoli Zinamon vodka
1/2 oz. cinnamon schnapps

Serve in chilled martini glass. Garnish with
cinnamon stick.

Debbie Wolklewicz
The Big Chill, Chattanooga, TN

Zorbatini Martini

1 1/2 oz. Stolichnaya vodka
1/4 oz. Metaxa ouzo

Stir gently with ice and strain. Garnish with a
green olive.

About the Author

Ray Foley has been a bartender for more than twenty years. He is the publisher of *Bartender* magazine and the author of *Bartending for Dummies* and *The Ultimate Little Shooter Book*. He has appeared on *Good Morning America*, *Live with Regis and Kathie Lee*, and countless other shows. Ray resides in New Jersey with his wife and partner, Jaclyn.